Contemporary Japanese Jewellery

Simon Fraser

MERRELL

in association with

Crafts Council

For my mother and father

This book has been produced to accompany the
exhibition *Contemporary Japanese Jewellery* at
Crafts Council Gallery
44a Pentonville Road
Islington
London N1 9BY
www.craftscouncil.org.uk
15 November 2001 – 13 January 2002

City Gallery
90 Granby Street
Leicester LE1 1DJ
22 January – 9 March 2002

Aberystwyth Arts Centre
Penglais
Aberystwyth SY23 3DE
3 April – 25 May 2002

First published 2001 by Merrell Publishers Limited

Distributed in the USA and Canada by Rizzoli
International Publications, Inc. through St Martin's
Press, 175 Fifth Avenue, New York, New York 10010

British Library Cataloguing-in-Publication Data:
Fraser, Simon
Contemporary Japanese jewellery
1.Jewelry – Japan 2.Jewelry – Japan – History –
20th century 3.Jewelers – Japan – Biography
I.Title II.Hida, Toyohiro
739.2'7'0952'09049

ISBN 1 85894 163 6

Produced by Merrell Publishers Limited
42 Southwark Street
London SE1 1UN

Designed by Karen Wilks
Edited by Iain Ross
Printed and bound in Italy

The Japan Foundation

The Satoh Artcraft Research & Scholarship Foundation

The Crafts Council is a registered charity
Registered charity number 280956

Front cover: Noriko Nagano, neckpiece,
urethane rubber
Back cover (left): Kimiaki Kageyama,
The Heart and *Suzushita*, brooches, 2001
(see pp. 58 and 59)
Back cover (right): Mizuko Yamada,
Breast Ornament, 1994 (see p. 110)
Page 1: Hiroyuki Mashiko, *Rouge*,
necklace, 1994 (see p. 67)
Page 2: Shinya Yamamura, *Brooch '98-12*,
1998 (see p. 118)

Contents

Foreword and Acknowledgements

This book accompanies the exhibition *Contemporary Japanese Jewellery*, curated by the British jeweller, tutor and writer Simon Fraser. The Crafts Council is delighted to participate in the UK's *Japan 2001* festival, intended to generate interest in all aspects of Japanese life, and has chosen to mark the occasion with a major project that offers a unique view on contemporary Japan and its applied arts. It is hoped that *Contemporary Japanese Jewellery* will encourage greater exchange between jewellers, collectors, scholars, curators, writers and enthusiasts in both countries, and inform a wider public of the vitality and innovation of work in the field.

In seeking to enable people to experience jewellery in its many manifestations, Simon Fraser has invented new conditions under which to view it, such as *Alchemy with a Piano* at the Institute of Contemporary Arts, London, in 1993, and his *Tattoo: A Day of Record* and performance entitled *Tremblant* at the Victoria and Albert Museum, London, in 2001. Together with his jewellery, these events have earned him a reputation as an iconoclast, but to accept this at face value would be to disregard the importance of the impact he has had as a facilitator of the work of practitioners who are 'unknown' or 'on the edge'. He is a passionate advocate of the eloquence of jewellery and the achievements of its pacesetters. Through curating this exhibition and writing this book he is again actively involved in communicating the experience of jewellery as an applied art form in all its subtlety and dynamism, bringing an inclusive selection of the work of fifty Japanese studio jewellers to the attention of the mainstream. This is the first time such a large number of Japanese jewellers has been gathered together.

Unlike the histories of jewellery in Europe and America, which are relatively well documented and exhibited, there has to date been insufficient study or exposure of Japanese jewellery to place it appropriately either within its own history or within the context of the international studio-jewellery movement. In 1995 the National Museum of Modern Art in Tokyo held a pioneering exhibition, *Contemporary Jewellery: Exploration by Thirty Japanese Artists*, to address exactly this situation, as noted by the museum's Director, Hiroshi Ueki. The exhibition denoted the acceptance of the discipline of jewellery into the art establishment. The accompanying catalogue, written by the museum's Curator for the Crafts Gallery and our Honorary Adviser, Toyojiro Hida, is therefore the key published source to date. Hida's text emphasizes the fine art of jewellery and is notable for its prescience in consolidating within Japan the identity of the studio-jewellery movement. Without this earlier project, the ambition to achieve a major survey of Japanese jewellery in Britain would have been unthinkable.

In the UK, certain exhibitions, notably *Japanese Contemporaries* at Lesley Craze Gallery, London, in 1997 and *Jewellery Moves* at the National Museums of Scotland, Edinburgh, in 1998, introduced audiences to the work of selected Japanese jewellers. *Contemporary Japanese Jewellery* represents a new contribution because it aims to provide a more substantial survey that identifies what is distinct about Japan and jewellery with historical references and that bridges the gap between Japanese jewellers and the contemporary international jewellery movement. Toyojiro Hida has addressed these questions from Japan, and his text provides an informative and questioning narrative to accompany the objects. Looking from a Western standpoint, Simon Fraser has been able to make new connections while nevertheless remaining mindful of the meanings embodied by materials and techniques and the context of a particular set of social codes and statuses.

Our warmest gratitude goes to all the jewellers represented in this exhibition, whose work has inspired everyone who has worked on the project. Special thanks go to our Honorary Adviser, Toyojiro Hida, Curator for the Crafts Gallery of the National Museum of Modern Art, Tokyo, for his essay and kind advice throughout the development of the exhibition. We are most grateful to Dr Senju Satoh and Katsuhiko Hayashi, President and Curator of the Satoh Artcraft Research and Scholarship Foundation, for financial and practical assistance in transporting the exhibits from Japan, and Mizuko Yamada, a jeweller based in Tokyo, for advice and assistance in structuring the exhibition. Special thanks are due to the Great Britain Sasakawa Foundation for funding; Junko Takekawa at the Japan Foundation; Jenny White at the British Council, London; and Takeshi Sakurai at the British Council, Tokyo, for encouragement and practical advice. I should also like to acknowledge and thank Jill Piercy for her support. Thanks are also due to Hajime Kimata and Reiko Yamada, President and former President of the Japan Jewellery Designers Association, Inc.; Professor Emeritus Yasuki Hiramatsu for advice and warm hospitality, and Ichiro Iino, Associate Professor, both of the Tokyo National University of Fine Arts and Music; and Takahiko Mizuno, President of Hiko Mizuno College of Jewellery, Tokyo. We are grateful to Merrell Publishers, who have produced this publication, and I should like to thank the exhibition designers Stickland Coombe for their creative and sensitive approach, as well as exhibition graphic designers Cartlidge Levine and NB: Studio for the design of publicity material. Finally, I should like to thank Simon Fraser for the curation of the exhibition and for his wonderful, informative catalogue essay, and the exhibition team at the Crafts Council: Louise Pratt, Julia Davies, Noriko Saito and Lisa Martin, and other colleagues who have supported and helped organize the project and associated events.

Dr Louise Taylor
Director of Exhibitions and Collection
Crafts Council
August 2001

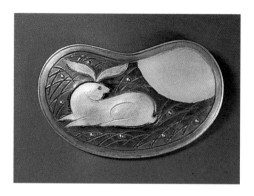

Mitsuo Masuda
see pp. 68–69

Masafumi Sekine
see p. 91

Noriko Nagano
see pp. 80–81

Cultural History of Personal Adornment in Japan
Simon Fraser

The history of jewellery in Japan is not only relatively unfamiliar to Western readers, but also to Japanese readers themselves. This history is only now being researched, and collectors are beginning to develop major holdings in the area. The text that follows, as I am well aware, gives only a cursory outline, which I have no doubt will become rapidly filled in and clarified as interest in this medium grows. As one would expect, practice surveyed over ten years displays a variety of approaches and ideas. The survey allows us to introduce a larger number of these ideas, examining long-standing trends and newer developments, rather than a partial view of that period of jewellery practice.

The culture of jewellery is an old one in Japan, notwithstanding an extensive break in its history. Archaeological excavations on Okinoshima Island in Fukuoka Prefecture have turned up gold rings from the sixth century AD, and, in Yamaguchi Prefecture, shell rings from the Yayoi period, which lasted from 250 BC until AD 300. Even older, a Jo-mon-period (7500–250 BC) or Iron Age ring, expertly carved in stone as a snake or a dragon biting its tail, has been discovered. There are links with parallel imagery in Hindu nagas and ancient Greek motifs.

When Japan converted aesthetically, socially and politically to Chinese style in the Nara period (AD 710–94), rings were dropped, as kimono and other courtly dress was not worn with rings or jewellery at all. The only jewellery-style items to be worn in any numbers during this time were hair combs, particularly elaborate ones evolving during the Edo period (1603–1868). Pieces of Western jewellery emerge from the next 400 years of Japanese history, evidence of a tiny thread of continuity, the result of trading during periods when Japan was open to outside influence and ideas. Trading was extensive right up until the seclusion of Japan in 1639, as traders were anxious to do business with Japan for many reasons; in particular, because of the superior quantities and quality of gold, silver and copper available. In exchange, notables hoarded Western luxuries such as Cordoba leather, fine glass ware, mirrors, clothes, candlesticks, foods and wines. None of the lists I have read so far refers specifically to jewellery, but it is likely that it was included.

The first substantial collection of jewellery to enter Japan appeared after the Meiji restoration in 1867. The 'modernization' or Westernization of Japan was a concerted attempt to enforce trade with the West, the abolition of feudal and other social structures and a refocusing of religious practice. An element of Japanese society embraced Western culture passionately in a manner that was to recur at intervals over the next 150 years.

Fashionability and novelty have a long social tradition in this culture, too. Rings and other forms of jewellery entered Japan as trade objects, gifts, curiosities and also as luxury items. Although the majority of these objects have disappeared, they can be seen in the Ukiyo-e or woodblock prints of the nineteenth century. Examples in the Kanji Hashimoto collection show the high-fashion styles of, perhaps, the water and willow worlds. The communities of geisha and upmarket hostesses created and consumed fashions in much the same way that the great courtesans of Paris were to patronize the couture house of Charles Worth, and as new items entered Japan, some were enthusiastically adopted. The woodblock prints in the collection, dating from 1878 until 1881, show possibly geisha (one woman is carrying a samisen) and rich fashionable women wearing bezel-set rings and other items alongside their kimonos. Watches and key chains were also worn to attach purses. Prints showing the upper half of the body allow enough space for the artist carefully to portray the rings, in one case reproducing the colour, red, and matching the colour of the woman's mouth with the ring, too, in case we might miss the detail. Consumption of such jewellery, either as import or as a Western-style object, showed modernity, fashionability and great luxury; indeed, such pieces might have been a gift from an influential patron.

Development of Artistic Jewellery as a Practice in Japan
The rich might have practised conspicuous consumption, but during this time Japan was undergoing a huge economic upheaval following the modernization. As part of this process, on 28 March 1876 (Meiji era 9), the right of samurai and other warrior classes to wear swords was abolished. This left swordsmiths and armour makers without work; the

lacquer market, supported by feudal lordships, collapsed; and the rise of Shinto as Japan's only religion left sculptors, chasers and casters of Buddhas out of work. The government embarked on a rigorous and forceful campaign to employ these craftsmen, with an export drive in arts and crafts. Exhibitions were organized, starting in 1877 with the first Domestic Industrial Exposition in Tokyo, to promote crafts, with prizes awarded in particular for skill. Japan began to present work abroad in the great nineteenth-century exhibitions, starting with the Philadelphia Centennial Exhibition of 1876 and the Exposition Universelle in Paris in 1878, and the second domestic exhibition was held in 1881. The problem remained that craftsmen who were used to chasing nail-head covers, ornamenting *tsuba* (sword guards) or inlaying steel needed to become aware of the items that were likely to be required internationally. So the government published a series of books, developed by officials, called *Onchi Zuroku* (Onchi Illustrations).

These pattern books, similar to the European tradition, represented the official line on good taste, suitable objects and motifs for craftsmen, and were rigorously promoted. Participants in the exhibitions were lent them to 'help' prepare for the events. Although *Onchi Zuroku* covered furniture and giftware (cigarette and cigar cases, pen boxes, blotters and so on) I do not know whether jewellery items were represented, though it would seem likely that they were.

Overseas visitors were also encouraged, called *oyatoi* (employees). Some, such as Christopher Dresser, who visited in 1876 for ninety-eight days, proved very valuable for the factories and workshops they visited. As we know, the experience was valuable for Dresser himself. By now items of Japanese craft exports had been on sale in London for a year in the Regent Street store of Arthur Lazenby Liberty.

Jewellery was quickly taken up by craftsmen as an area of manufacture. A key figure in its development was Manzaburo Matsumura, who trained in chasing and metalwork, finishing his apprenticeship at the age of twenty-three in 1873. He started a workshop making copies of imported jewellery and exploring new designs of his own. Working with apprentices, he was already supplying the empress and others by 1878, and exhibited seventeen items (rings and buttons) in the government industrial exhibition. The success of enterprises such as Matsumura's is reflected in the fact that by the third domestic exhibition in 1890 crafts of an original design only were accepted, not those of the *Onchi Zuroku*. Matsumura's workshops experimented with melting and casting platinum, at that point unknown in Japan, and he went on to build a business employing dozens of craftsmen in five factories, opening his own shop in Kodenmachou by 1888. Advisers to the Matsumura business used their expertise to help the growth of two fledgling early twentieth-century businesses, Mikimoto Pearls and the watch company Hattori Seiko, contributing to the framework of these highly successful jewellery giants.

By 1887 schools of arts and music set up to encourage skills and the development of ideas were amalgamated into institutions such as the Tokyo National University of Fine Arts and Music, also called Geidai. Gradually, universities grew in different cities in Japan, and these have preserved and nurtured traditional skills right up to the present day, keeping alive crafts and skills that had been threatened by 'modernization'.

During the 1920s and 1930s some sections of Japanese society embraced modernity with fervour, joining the vogue for dances and cocktails. Rich socialites wore dresses by or inspired by Parisian designers, teamed with jewellery in Art Deco styles. This was a period of profound self-questioning in Japan; even the fabled geisha came under attack as old-fashioned, and suggestions were made that they should modernize (for which read Westernize) their dress. There was also discussion about the value of different elements of traditional costumes, objects and customs, and the skills associated with them.

The writings of the philosopher Soetsu Yanagi (1889–1961), who was devoted to collecting and preserving folk-craft traditions, developed into a movement called Mingei, which was defined by its opposition to bourgeois fine art. Celebrating everyday objects made by nameless but skilled craftsmen, indispensable but affordably priced, Mingei created a powerful ideology within the applied arts. This was promoted in the work of the potters Shoji Hamada and, in Britain, Bernard Leach, among others. The moral undercurrent of the movement, its idealism and the resulting artworks were to attract makers both in Japan and in Britain.

Mitsuo Masuda and fellow students, 1930s

The fusion of traditional craft skills – used originally for a specific purpose – in a simple, understated object can be seen in the work exhibited by Mitsuo Masuda. Masuda was one of a group of metal craftsmen who trained at the Tokyo National University of Fine Arts and Music in the 1930s. The group included Shiro Naitoh, Toshihiko Gotoh and Sakuji Wakabayashi. Masuda can be seen (left) among other important jewellers, bent over his work. This was a very interesting time to train in the applied arts, as the Nippon Mingeikan, the folk arts museum, was to open in Tokyo in 1936. Masuda started his practice around this time after a training that had been framed by the knowledge that the schools had sustained since the 'modernization' of the nineteenth century. So clear is this line that one of the first pieces of jewellery that Masuda crafted – an example of this type of object from 1936 is included in the catalogue – was a chased, square, nail-head cover for a sword, made from silver and crisply executed, both front and back, revealing the level of craftsmanship. The shank is simply two wires soldered in parallel and fixed to the sides of the cover. As a ring it has a bold, almost Art Deco quality, square with a strong decorative pattern. It is a short step from nail cover to jewellery, something recognized among practitioners at the time.

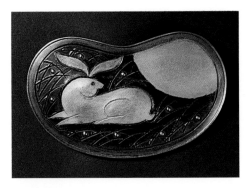

Mitsuo Masuda
see pp. 68–69

This one-step process is clearly not the case with all of the jewellery objects made either by Masuda or his contemporaries, but it does provide an important link between future jewellery practice and traditional craft skills. Taste for particular craft skills was affected by the espousal of utilitarian, ordinary or normal things by Mingei, which allowed a duality of thought process to develop where the anonymous craft object, admired for its beauty, develops alongside the named artists' works, which have an importance and influence. Certainly, within Japanese metalwork, different techniques occupy different levels of status and value, and attract different levels of connoisseurship and scholarship. The work of Masuda and others was to bring to the fore the chasing technique of *keri bori*, or 'kick carving', among others. A simple, fast, line-making process, the marks it leaves on the metal are fresh and unsophisticated, and especially graphic in quality. Masuda used this technique to draw on metal when creating imagery, developing a leaven for richer and more formal techniques. The result was a lightness, a visually delicate object, more easily wearable than the group of techniques could apparently allow. The group of makers with which Masuda was associated changed tastes and the status of such techniques. Masuda was recognized by the title 'Living National Treasure' (properly 'Important Intangible Cultural

Property') in recognition of his knowledge, marking a career that included many domestic metal objects as well as jewellery pieces. He provides a link to the present, because, as I write, he is still, at the age of ninety-two, actively making jewellery.

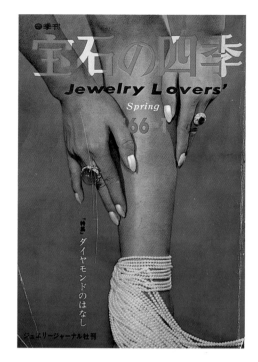

Post-war Japan proved to be a different place, and great efforts were made by the industrial jewellery manufacturers to promote diamonds and an international style of jewellery. Artist-jewellers initially responded to this by forming the Ur Accessories Association, named after the astonishing ancient gold finds, a title later modified to the Ur Jewellery Association, a political change signalling a more confident attitude (traditionally, accessories – for example, for women's hair – were not considered important as works of art). The group was started by members of the *chokin* department at Geidai in 1956: Shiro Naitoh, who by then was Professor; Toshihiko Gotoh, Assistant Professor; and Yasuhiko Hishida, who went on to become the first professor at the Musashino Art College, an influential private fine-arts college. The Ur group was intended to formalize an interest in developing jewellery that used traditional Japanese sword-manufacturing techniques of chasing, coloured metals and inlays, among others. Holding formal exhibitions and printing catalogues, the group continues today to demonstrate its members' strong interest in precious metals, traditional techniques and unusual stones, clear evidence of its founders' passions.

Four Seasons of Jewellery, **spring 1966**
Jewellery Journal Co. Ltd

In 1963 a different organization was set up: the Japan Jewellery Designers Association (JJDA), originally begun by Yasuhiko Hishida, who became the first president of the board, Koji Iwakura, Kyoko Ikeda, Kazuko Shino and nineteen other jewellers. Members such as Yasuki Hiramatsu and Reiko Yamada were to become pillars of the jewellery world in the following decades. The written manifesto marks the point at which jewellers started to recognize that to create a market and recognition for their work within Japan, they would have to change the way language was used. Jewellery was still seen as a fashion accessory. Annual exhibitions allowed the presentation of members' work and also the publication of catalogues that present a useful pictorial history of the development of Japanese jewellery during this time. The organization received a fillip when it was featured in a new magazine launched in 1965. *Four Seasons of Jewellery* was started by the Jewellery Journal Co. Ltd., with Noriko Takagi as editor. Takagi, still editor of *Four Seasons* among other publications, has recorded the history of artists' jewellery alongside developments across the commercial jewellery world, in Japan and internationally. Placing the work of artists next to designers for industry and jewellery focused on the presentation of stones and important brand names. Even the English translation of the name for such jewellers, 'high-fancy jewellers', conveys something of the mood. Jewellery designers in Japan view themselves as participants in this duality; certainly, it has become accepted practice to choose a career trajectory that might embrace both training as an artist and designing for the market. Sometimes big names in each field originally trained together and remain friends. *Four Seasons of Jewellery* reflects this divide but has continued to present the work of both areas alongside each other. The work of Yasuki Hiramatsu and Reiko Yamada, for instance, as illustrated in the photographs of 1965, can be seen to demonstrate the themes that are still evident in their work today: Hiramatsu's formal, abstract interest in line and texture within volumes of metal, and Yamada's preoccupation with space and frameworks as a vehicle for precious stones and imagery.

Jewellers in Japan were starting to become more informed about developments in Europe and Scandinavia during the 1960s. In 1961 Graham Fuller of Goldsmiths' Hall in London

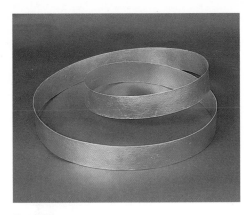

Yasuki Hiramatsu
See pp. 54–55

Reiko Yamada
See pp. 112–13

curated a landmark artists' jewellery exhibition. Covering the period 1861–1961, it included historical and contemporary artists' jewellery and, importantly, some of the new, younger jewellery artists. Long recognized as a significant event in European post-war jewellery, the exhibition reached Japan in 1965, and was presented at the dynamic Seibu department store's internal exhibition space, to great interest. Japanese department stores are exciting places with an all-encompassing quality. Providing customers with a bewildering choice of consumer goods, they also offer spaces for eating, drinking and relaxation. Exhibition galleries present a busy schedule of arts and social events, from international fine art to bonsai award exhibitions. These shows are often of short duration, but this allows a rapid turnover, and during the 1960s and 1970s many jewellers were kept up to date by such exhibitions. The network of small, formal jewellery galleries – sometimes devoted to jewellery, sometimes to applied arts in general – that flourishes now was not yet available. The catalogues produced allowed the dissemination of information into the jewellery community. Jewellery from Britain, for example, was shown right up to the 1970s as part of mixed-group shows presented by the British Crafts Centre. Indeed, jewellers such as Gerda Flockinger were making sales right from the beginning. This exhibition policy meant shows from all over the world reached Japan and provided diverse information.

In 1970 a major change took place in exhibitions with the first International Jewellery Art Exhibition, organized by the JJDA. Despite the influx of influences and ideas from abroad, however, it was still taken for granted "that jewellery, even in its independence, had to remain harmonious with the fashion for clothes". In his catalogue entry for the *Contemporary Jewellery* exhibition of 1995, Toyojiro Hida discusses the influence of the assimilation of fine-art practices into international jewellery movements and the effect on work in Japan from the late 1970s onwards. That jewellery could be seen and appreciated as small-scale sculpture was immediately understood in a culture that produced objects such as netsuke, and, furthermore, it allowed jewellers publicly to move jewellery away from its socially inferior position as "only a woman's ornaments". The second point he makes is more important. The overt self-expression evident in international work struck a chord, as such personally driven work is characteristic of the wider field of post-war applied arts in Japan. There is, of course, self-expression evident within post-war contemporary jewellery; however, this external indicator seems to have meant that jewellers finally felt that they could join this arena as equals, and a wider Japanese society was able to appreciate this. At last jewellers were able to change the status of jewellery within Japanese culture. Such a formal repositioning in a culture where status is very important should not be underestimated, for an appropriate status makes the engagement of viewers in the wider population a more comfortable and social experience. It also allows official recognition, which was marked by Toyojiro Hida's exhibition of 1995 at the Museum of Modern Art in Tokyo.

During the 1980s and early 1990s the flow of information continued between jewellers inside and outside Japan through the format of the International Jewellery Art Exhibitions. Prizes were awarded to international exhibitors that included Gianpaolo Babetto, Joel Brakman and Graziano Visintin in 1983, Franceso Pavan, Tone Viglund and Verena Siber-Fuchs, who won the grand prize in 1986. That her torn-paper necklace should win was a shock to some Japanese jewellers. By 1991 Japanese jewellers were exhibiting their work in Europe, and in particular in Norway, where the JJDA organized a group show of its makers. This re-examination of materials as part of the European and wider contemporary jewellery movement was to find a resonance in the work produced in Japan. The physicality and nature of materials is still very much appreciated as a general part of Japanese culture. This we can see extended right through the history of Japanese domestic and public material cultures. Even today, for younger Japanese, this is true, and can in part explain the enthusiasm for new materials and processes that has characterized the booming consumer market of the past twenty years. By now Japanese jewellers were starting to have an impact on the wider world stage, joining other schools in Europe and America as part of an international dialogue. From 1993 the Three Schools Project had been running, initiated by Otto Kunzli of the Akademie der Bildenden Künste in Munich; it was a joint project that led to an exhibition and a book.

The Three Schools Project united the Munich and the Amsterdam Reitveld academies with the Hiko Mizuno College of Jewellery in Tokyo. Among the most ambitious and dynamic of the many private schools of jewellery, the Hiko Mizuno operates from its own purpose-built base in downtown Tokyo. The late Kazuhiro Itoh, Head of Jewellery and a jeweller interested in conceptual frameworks, made strong international links, and had a strong impact on a generation of students. The influence of this European way of thinking can be seen in the work of Yudai Nakabayashi, who took part, and Teruo Akatsu and Shinichiro Kobayashi, who formed part of the same generation. Within the practice of such jewellery, interrogation of culture as practised in Europe becomes more a reflection upon culture, a matter of indicators and material signifiers rather than of direct cultural criticism. Teruo Akatsu's roof-tile pieces are an example of these, remaking an item with religious and emotive home ties into a neckpiece of delicacy and elegance. The definition of the neckpiece by the wave of the roof-tile form is subsumed into the finished piece almost unnoticeably.

Review of Contemporary Jewellery in Japan

During the 1990s the numbers of jewellers continued to grow. Today, learning the skills of jewellery in Japan can be accomplished in a variety of different ways, and in each case jewellers bring different approaches and information to the field. Formal training in either metalworking or jewellery techniques can be obtained by studying full time at universities and vocational colleges across Japan, with part-time and evening courses also available. Prospective jewellers can join classes based in established jewellers' workshops. This atelier system, focused on the skills and knowledge of a senior and respected maker, not only provides an income for the maker but also allows those studying to learn as quickly or as slowly as they like. Some professional jewellers are women who originally began to learn jewellery as a hobby and then turned semi- or fully professional. Some Japanese travel abroad to learn, bringing back attitudes and skills new to Japan. Traditional skills in lacquer or *cloisonné* enamel, historically associated with objects and furniture, are put to use.

Attendance at classes for jewellery is growing and diversifying, and Japanese pop culture is even starting to influence this trend, with younger male pop stars wearing jewellery, boosting applications from male students. The different schooling systems provide different opportunities and are perceived as having different status levels. The atelier system of study can work extremely well, with a group of artists developing around one venue. In the long term this has mitigated against the perception of jewellery as an art form among other practitioners, as the many women attendees reinforce gender prejudices and obstruct a clear examination of the quality of the work.

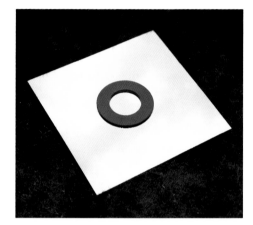

Hiroyuki Mashiko
See p. 67

Teruo Akatsu
See p. 39

Masafumi Sekine
See p. 91

This diversity of approaches is reflected in the items selected for this exhibition and catalogue, and the jewellery of fifty makers offers a starting point from which to look at what defines Japanese jewellery at this time. Most work produced is located firmly within the boundaries of traditional jewellery objects, formats common in artists' jewellery of the twentieth century: rings, brooches, earrings, pendants and so on. The influence of the European exploration of body-centred ornament is less felt, even though significant numbers of jewellers were already working at this time and the influence of the Modernist jewellery project can be seen on Japanese jewellery as a whole. I would argue that this is not necessarily the result of a failure to understand such work, or, indeed, ignorance of it, but indicates a particular approach to the incorporation of jewellery into Japanese dress during a long period of Westernization.

A brooch is an object that is attached to clothes rather than touching the body (a non-traditional situation), so it is perhaps the object that Japanese culture has adopted most easily. It also fits with the notion of jewellery as a sculptural object or, even more clearly in some cases, as a pictorial surface; the work of Masafumi Sekine is clearly equally balanced between both. The formal framework of an object, within which the artist's voice can be articulated through manipulation of technique, subject-matter and artistic innovation, is something with which many makers feel comfortable. That the artist feels confident allows the wearer or client to involve themselves too. This framework also allows something else to happen that is important to the area of work as a whole. With artists forced to develop ideas within structures, a form of pressure builds up, consisting of demands upon the maker to fulfil social and self-imposed criteria within the framework of the piece. This creates objects, many examples of which are in the exhibition and catalogue, that have an intensity, a concentrated quality about them that could be said to be characteristic of this period of work – an intensity so palpable as to have a tangible quality, differing in flavour or mood between jewellers. The methodical approach to working both through technique and in pursuit of a mood or atmosphere favoured by many makers could be part of the root of this. Another is the generally high level of technical prowess, something that is well regarded in general by artists. Many makers bring a deep understanding of their material and its possibilities to their work, and are precise about the positioning of the work through this selection.

Technical expertise lies at the root of much jewellery made in Japan, either within the field of artists' jewellery or that of the wider commercial world; however, jewellery is becoming unique in the way that its traditional techniques can find new relevance to contemporary Japanese society. *Urushi*, or lacquer, for example, is originally a Chinese technique, practised in Japan since the Heian period of 794–1192 when it became thoroughly incorporated. The lacquer artist working today is presented with a medium that is associated with particular values, identities and, in some cases, particular objects for particular purposes. Not all of these objects, however exquisite, have any relevance to contemporary society, or indeed a market among younger Japanese, the peers of the makers. Jewellery, however, allows makers the freedom to explore new possibilities outside the more strictly controlled models and also to offer a new approach exploiting traditional skills. Parallel to this runs the use of traditional motifs in a society to which visual iconography is very important. The iconography that makers are willing to incorporate into their work sometimes seems surprising. It is impossible to imagine a future Japan without such iconography, and the *sakura* is a good case in point. Cherry-blossom season in major cities is heralded by street lamps and awnings sprouting a range of neon-coloured plastic cherry blossoms, a practice that is becoming almost a tradition in itself. Not natural at all, they provide a suitably festive response to the dense urbanity of modern Japan. Even within jewellery such iconography persists, as artists attempt to modernize these elements and apply them within their work.

The ebb and flow of Japan's interest in other cultures is characterized within Japanese society by a passionate, enthusiastic and academic fascination with art, science or business. Just as familiar after a period of time is the sense among a group dynamic that there should be a return to informing Japanese culture with the new haul of information. This information is then quietly and clearly absorbed into Japanese culture and 'japonized'. Such a translation of cultural ideas and practice has as its corollary the same mechanism in Western Europe. One of the most famous of the mechanisms was the use of Ukiyo-e, or Japanese woodblock prints, by the Impressionists to give new forms of perspective to the Western painting tradition. For jewellery, an import in its own right, the gaze has for some time been an outward one, but the increasing inclusion of traditional Japanese techniques would seem to signify more than the start of an inward-looking period. The Japanese tradition of exploring materials, in fact the material diversity of Japanese cultural objects, from the highly materially valuable to the highly valued culturally – not, of course, always the same thing – is one that is still fundamental to the consumption of goods. Because jewellery does not have a formalized purpose in Japanese society it offers the makers of 'culture' in Japan an opportunity for immense freedom. The use of traditional techniques is not so much a withdrawal as a realization of the possibilities inherent in the "jewellery project".

The opportunity to investigate materials exposed the value of traditional knowledge bases. It is not that some makers do not find satisfaction and comfort in working with traditional techniques in the face of Japan's notorious contemporary cultural speed. This premise is familiar to us in the development of European applied arts, where just as a craft is dying it becomes adopted by more self-conscious practitioners and moves up the social scale and price bracket. The aesthetic of the temporary, at its most familiar in the manifestation of *sakura*, or cherry-blossom season, a point of temporary perfection and beauty soon to vanish, brings with the choice of materials a familiarity with something only valuable at a certain time, when utilized in a particular manner. The very abstractness of the Modernist appropriation of material in jewellery allows its reappropriation for other, more traditionally loaded metaphors. The position that makers take on the historical information available and the development of contemporary work is necessarily a personal one. Deciding what to make and how it will be received is a constant dilemma, regardless of culture or practice. However, makers are also prey to ambition; some intend work for internal domestic consumption, others have wider and more international ambitions. Strategies for framing ideas for international or traditional consumption, as part of the wider jewellery dialogue or even as a fusion of all three are represented by work in this exhibition and catalogue. Reaching out from a culture can be an exciting and perilous procedure, and it is clear that those jewellers with a keen sense of foreign perceptions of Japan are more immediately successful. Particularly exciting, however, are those jewellers who bring very Japanese ways of thinking to making jewellery that transcends culture and practice. Ritsuko Ogura's corrugated-cardboard work is perhaps a case in point. Paper has a long history of being an extremely valuable material in Japan, and is still vibrantly contemporary in its applications.

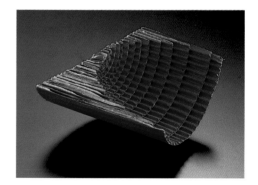

Ritsuko Ogura
See p. 90

Minato Nakamura
See pp. 84–85

Takashi Koyama
See p. 66

Ogura's almost Mingei-like exploration of the poetics of corrugated cardboard lends her jewellery a strong impact that speaks well internationally.

Across the range of work included here, it is also possible to determine other, less immediately obvious characteristics. Many brooches and other items are flat. Graphic images or surface detailing are often presented in this way. Indeed, fine-art painting in Japan was historically two-dimensional. The representation of a landscape on, for example, a screen, did not use perspective as in the West; instead, the foreground was indicated by the bottom of the image, distance by the top. The result was a flat graphic pattern, and, as the jewellery shows, this is still an important and valuable method for artists.

The simplest way to create three dimensions from a flat surface is to fold it. Folding is an element of Japanese culture that is, in the form of origami, accorded the status of an art form. The folds in a kimono can indicate who the wearer is and, after some time, make it impossible for that kimono to be refolded to be worn by someone of a different status. Many makers have chosen to use folding, or a fold, to create three dimensions or to embellish surfaces. The fold is represented in many different materials: Nobuko Nishiwaki offers delicate unfolded forms carved, surprisingly, from white marble, while Minato Nakamura uses it fluidly, and Nagi Nakajima strengthens her sheet metal with repeat folds. Takashi Koyama folds metal by cutting, allowing curves to create light chains from the sheet, and for Noriko Nagano it is the very fluidity and foldability of rubber that drives her whole project.

Sometimes Japanese jewellery can appear familiar to Western viewers, as we recognize ideas or techniques or even physicalities. There is, I suppose, an expectation that all jewellery from Japan, coming as it does from such a distinctive culture, should appear very unfamiliar indeed. Research into and exploration of jewellery conducted by the Japanese over the past 100 years, and the incorporation of jewellery into their culture, an exercise that was originally tentative, have now combined, gathering speed as a movement in its own right. Transcribed into Japanese culture, ideas are starting to break free from their original modes of representation, providing a rich and fertile ground for possibilities. Contemporary Japanese jewellery can be characterized by an interest in skill and the techniques of material manipulation, a wide-ranging and versatile approach to old and new materials, clear, individual makers' voices, an interest in change and novelty, and an expectation of wearability that allows for general social participation in the project. Makers are producing strong and exciting pieces that are already, and increasingly will be, recognized by the international jewellery community. They are realized through a combination of core jewellery ideas, Japanese cultural viewpoints and the opportunity that jewellery affords creative makers in Japan today. The interface between Japanese makers and the practice of jewellers worldwide is almost complete, and I hope *Contemporary Japanese Jewellery* contributes to that. Confidence is high.

Circumventing Modernism: Japanese Jewellery of the 1990s
Toyojiro Hida

1

I should like to start with an artist named Mikiko Minewaki.

It is not that I know much about her, apart from the fact she was born in Akita Prefecture in 1967, studied jewellery-making at the Hiko Mizuno College of Jewellery in Shibuya, Tokyo, from 1985 to 1989, and currently teaches there. But the first time I saw her work, it made a very strong impression on me and very effectively communicated what this artist's attitude towards jewellery is.

Mikiko Minewaki, *Plapetal 'Zoi'*, 1997–98

I still remember the occasion clearly. It was in 1996, in a show at the Gallery Obra Vida in Shibuya. Minewaki's work was distinctly different from that of other artists of her generation. It seemed, above all, totally indifferent to attracting attention, given that here was an emerging artist who was trying to win recognition. It was a necklace made of innumerable small pieces of plastic cut out with a jigsaw and strung together with thin nylon cords (see left). The plastic pieces came from a variety of ordinary objects: a bowl, an ice tray, a mobile phone, a calculator, toy and a spoon. Each of the pieces was slim and slightly curved. They had a certain beauty in their fragility, but, being made of plastic, they did not have very much appeal in themselves. Minewaki still works in the same style today.

The slim fragments of plastic she uses remind me of bitten-off fingernails. The actual plastic pieces, however, are clean, and she takes such pleasure in the very act of cutting those innumerable fragments out of plastic things that she becomes totally absorbed in the repetition of the task and oblivious to the world outside.

In recent years, social withdrawal has become a widespread phenomenon in Japan: people who cannot cope well in society stop going to school or the office, and go into a long period of shutting themselves in their rooms. This is partly due to mental illness, but it has also become a social phenomenon that epitomizes today's Japan. Minewaki's making of plastic fragments seems to reflect this mental attitude: socially withdrawn individuals, by secluding themselves, show only that they cannot fit into school or society; they do not have the will to change that school or society. In Minewaki's case, too, the repeated process is not a means to bring about change in existing jewellery design, but is a goal in itself. To what end does she make these fragments? What meaning is there in the work assembled from them? Minewaki's works seem totally unconcerned by such questions.

When one imagines her, totally absorbed in her actions as she cuts out these plastic pieces, working without any premeditated goal or pattern, one is tempted to consider her to be denouncing the modern preoccupation with the self. But it soon becomes plain that Minewaki does not intend such a thing. In order to understand her work, it is necessary first to depart from the widely accepted view that, in works of jewellery, seminal concepts precede all processes of actual making, though it is also true that her works do not embody conventional concepts either.

According to the artist herself, Minewaki has chosen to work with plastic fragments to show that jewellery can be made from ordinary, mass-produced materials. In making this statement, she does not criticize, as junk art has done, the self-bestowed supremacy of fine art; instead, her work is an expression of her appreciation of ordinary, everyday activities and the values that are based on them.

Created according to such precepts, Minewaki's jewellery stands in direct opposition to Modernism, which emphasizes originality of expression and form, as well as the uniqueness of each work of art. More precisely, she remained uninfluenced by the Modernist trend in Japanese jewellery of the 1980s, staying aloof from its emphasis on artistic purity, originality and creativity. What lies at the basis of her work is a constant and determined desire to continue creating pieces of jewellery, even when there is no central concept to support the act theoretically.

2

This attitude – creating jewellery for the satisfaction to be found in the making process rather than in pursuit of innovative artistic expression – is widely found in the Japanese jewellery of the past decade. The creative impulse is not focused towards a goal; it is diffused throughout the process. In the 1990s, many new artists entered the field of jewellery in Japan, but they seem to be unsure of where they are going.

There have been attempts to give new purposes and meanings to jewellery, but they have failed to become established in the Japanese cultural climate. One example is the jewellery competition held by the Austrian crystal glass manufacturer Swarovski in 1996, 1997 and 1998. The event was, of course, part of the firm's marketing project in Japan, but, at least in the 1997 competition, the organizers clearly expressed a desire to revise the image of jewellery held by the Japanese. Vivienne Becker, who served as the head of the judges for the occasion, described the theme for that year's competition as follows:

Swarovski Japan has selected 'Street Pride' as the theme of the first fashion jewellery competition it holds on its own in Japan. This is a theme which reflects the importance of youth culture in Japan and the influence it has on contemporary fashion and lifestyle. Street fashion has internationally become a significant social phenomenon in the past fifty years, and has expressed itself most notably in clothing and accessories. In Japan, particularly, the rich cultural background has enabled young people to create very original and distinctive styles. (Catalogue of Swarovski Design Competition, 1997)

Talking about street style here, Becker, who lives in London, probably had in mind the counterculture that became a prevalent force among the youth of Britain in the 1970s. It produced punk fashion and punk rock, but it also embodied the conflicts that existed between different generations and between the working class and the rich. Particularly in the Camden area of London, one can still see today somewhat modified versions of the gaudy and aggressive street fashions that once embodied the discontent of young people shut out of the social circles of the rich and powerful. Becker would not have expected this same structure of social conflicts to have existed in Japan, but she seems to have assumed that Japanese youth also felt itself part of a similar social conflict. It is likely that, having seen young people in Tokyo weirdly and outrageously dressed, she assumed that it was a kind of self-assertion that originated with some form of social conflict, and chose the title 'Street Pride' for the competition.

But in the 1990s, or even today, did the young people of Japan have something to fight against, confronting a social pressure that would crush them if they stopped asserting themselves?

3

PRETTY FOR SURVIVAL!

Komako Nihonmatsu, *Pretty for Survival!*, Swarovski
Design Competition catalogue, 1997

Komako Nihonmatsu's *Pretty for Survival!* (left), which won the Best Drawing Award in the second Swarovski Design Competition in Japan, seems to provide an answer to this question. This design featured a huge heart-shaped ornament to be worn upon the buttocks, but what was crucial about it was not the ornament's size but the fact that it was shown being worn by a girl dressed in a senior-high-school uniform. Until a few years ago, girls of this age generally wore their uniform skirts very short and donned long, very loose-fitting white socks, this being their preferred fashion. The sailor-collar uniform and the white socks were, in their original forms as set down in the school rules, very conservative and discreet. The young girls modified them in small rebellions against their teachers and parents. But when the modified styles became prevalent, they lost any rebellious connotations.

Another thing that was associated with girls of this age was 'dating for financial support', which was in reality a form of prostitution. The girls agreed to 'date' older men in return for 'financial support': cash. Of course, only a small percentage of this age group actually engaged in such acts, but this kind of 'dating' seems nevertheless to have been fairly widespread. It was not an unusual practice confined to dropouts.

Girls who dressed in very short skirts and loose-fitting white socks, refusing to fit into the image of the modest and obedient girl, were actually trying to become self-sufficient and independent. In Nihonmatsu's work, the large ornament is worn not on the breast or the hand but on the buttocks, emphasizing that this girl is sexual merchandise. I understood her drawing to be a cynical self-portrait. In giving it the title *Pretty for Survival!*, she apparently feels some kinship with the young girls who no longer find it totally abhorrent to sell themselves for financial independence. These young girls were trying to gain greater power in society through casting off the image of well-protected girlhood. Did they have to fight against any specific group or social pressure? The modifications in dress that were originally a form of rebellion soon became a fashion; 'financial-support dating' was not only for the poor. There was nothing specific to fight for. If they were actually fighting against anything at all, it was the stereotypical images of the modest student or the young female as sexual merchandise that existed in society.

The ideas and images shared by the members of a society are never clearly defined. They are formed out of the social climate, and turn into established and acknowledged facts even before people become aware of them. Such accepted images tend to have extensive power over individuals in Japan because, for one thing, we do not have distinct social classes. When everyone is given a chance to succeed, social and ideological conflicts are rare. What is felt as a far more immediate defining force by the young is fashion, which must stay within certain accepted ranges. The rules of taste are never clearly delineated, but the young are always conscious of them. In the constant effort to follow the invisible rules they share, they rarely get far enough actually to rebel against anything; what appear to be rebellious acts are usually nothing more than the trappings of fashion.

Unfamiliar with the social and cultural situation in Japan, the people at Swarovski Crystal took the unruly fashions of Japanese youth as an expression of rebellious pride, and chose this as the theme for their competition. Nihonmatsu succeeded in addressing this ineffective theme by approaching it side-on and expressing the young girls' suppressed need for freedom in a cynical way. It seems to be expected that the Japanese should be very ardent protectors of their own culture, but they are often just as good at fulfilling what is expected of them by foreigners.

4

Besides Modernist trends, Japanese jewellery has been exposed to another external influence that might have introduced 'purpose' and 'meaning' to it: silver jewellery of rugged design, originally meant to be worn by men. The most popular motifs are Celtic patterns, crosses, skulls and chains, which in Western culture are associated with medieval or pagan religious rites, the primitive lifestyles of indigenous peoples, or the great rise of rock music after the War: they embody, in the West, a determination on young people's parts to remain unassimilated by the Establishment. In that sense, this kind of silver jewellery is a subcategory of the street jewellery that was born with the subculture. The best-known brand is Chrome Hearts, but similar pieces are produced in many Western countries.

This type of silver jewellery was introduced to Japan in the late 1980s, detached from its original associations with paganism or native peoples. It became popular among people in their late teens. In this particular age group, it was far more popular than contemporary jewellery with its refined designs. But as they spread further among Japanese youth, these silver accessories lost the rebellious connotations they had originally had. To be widely adopted in Japan, they had to be modified and diluted so that wearing them would not mean falling out of that accepted range of taste the young people adhered to. As a result, silver jewellery in Japan has become an accessory with no aggressive message: even in its most eloquent mode, it is nothing more than a sign used as part of self-assertion.

Going through Chrome Hearts's Japanese brochure, one realizes that the company considers its main target to be not the young, but middle-aged men enjoying both free time and financial stability. Its message seems to be that silver jewellery is not only for the young, but also for every man who lives a life of his own. But what exactly is a life that is one's own? Perhaps it is the small details that set one apart from the rest. Or perhaps it means having one's own opinions. To a student or a corporate manager, to the affluent or the worker, silver jewellery can carry the same meaning in Japan. This again seems to indicate that Japanese society has an unusually uniform structure without social hierarchy. As street jewellery became a recognized fashion, contemporary jewellery in the conventional style gradually lost the significance it had in the 1980s as an experimental art form.

Reflecting this tendency, the Japan Jewellery Designers Association (JJDA) stopped holding large-scale international competitions after its International Jewellery Art Exhibition of 1986, and in the 1990s held only member exhibitions and domestic competitions on alternate years. Though its decision to stop holding international competitions was due to the financial circumstances that accompanied the general slowing down of the Japanese economy, in making it JJDA gave up its rôle of disseminator to the world of the latest trends in Japanese jewellery. The members of the association were now on their own in their explorations of artistic expression. And yet, even after the JJDA stopped making aesthetic statements as a group, the number of jewellery artists who participated in its competitions steadily increased: it was 162 in 1992; 194 in 1996; 195 in 1998; and 212 in 2000. And in the open competition for everyday tools held by the Japan Craft Design Association there has been a rapid increase in the number of participants in the field of jewellery: it was 51 in 1991; 70 in 1995; and 124 in 2000. How can we explain this?

In 1995, an exhibition of contemporary jewellery that featured Japanese work from the first half of the 1990s was held at the National Museum of Modern Art, Tokyo. It included both artists who in the early 1980s started to incorporate sculptural composition in their work, and those who in the late 1980s began to explore ways of deconstructing the very concept of jewellery. The works of the latter group were more adventurous and interesting. The central figure among them was Kazuhiro Itoh. Under his influence, Hiroyuki Mashiko made a necklace that was a torus-shaped mass of lipstick to show that one of the most fundamental functions of jewellery is that of adding colour to the human body.

But this group's attempts to re-examine the concept of jewellery no longer look very valid. One of the reasons is Itoh's death in 1997; his artistic theories and strategies had been the group's driving force. Nevertheless, these attempts had to lose their impetus sooner or later, since they were, in spite of the boldness of their experimentation, also based very much on lyrical appeal. I still wonder for what purpose and for whom the deconstruction of jewellery was attempted. Though I was involved in the mounting of that contemporary jewellery exhibition, I have not found a satisfactory reason for the disappearance of such innovation from the field.

5

Japanese jewellery of the 1990s was unable to find new purposes or meanings. But as an art form it enjoyed a steady growth, with street jewellery becoming popular among young people, and more and more artists taking part in open competitions.

This general growth in the face of a lack of central focus would certainly seem strange to those outside Japan; the situation seems paradoxical even to me, watching it unfold from the inside. But it was pointed out about 100 years ago by the Austrian poet–critic Ernst Schur that Japanese art is an art of the senses, based on emotional and sensory elements. In comparison to Western art, which can be considered an art of the mind, dominated by theories and ideas, Japanese art appears to lack a theoretical backbone. We must bear in mind that Schur ascribed these contrasting characteristics to Japanese and Western art in an attempt, as a participant of the Vienna Secession movement, to analyse what made Japanese art different, and he naturally tended to make assumptions and exaggerate. However, most Japanese do feel that Japanese art has a tendency to capture human situations through instinct and inspiration rather than logic and theory.

Schur likens the Japanese mentality that forms the basis of all Japanese art to plant life:

The life of the Japanese is like that of a plant. They seem to feel that their existence is connected to something eternal. Their awareness lacks animal will. And yet they do not seem to be clearly aware that they have very acute senses. To us Europeans, plant life seems too monotonous and alien. We will never find satisfaction in such a petty existence ...

A Japanese has said: "I go to the woods and watch a beetle crawling across a grass leaf and get fascinated by strange-shaped clouds. I look at bodies of mist passing through trees far down toward the bottom of the valley. Immersed in these natural scenes, I feel my soul tremble." (From Ernst Schur, 'Japanische Kunst', retranslated from the Japanese version by Shinsuke Tanimoto in *Ver Sacrum*, April 1899)

This passage recalls how Mikiko Minewaki finds pleasure in simply cutting out plastic fragments. One hundred years after Schur made this observation, the Japanese perhaps still lack animal will, finding contentment in the small things in life.

As Schur pointed out, the Japanese lead lives that are directed more by the senses than the will. But even so, can works of Japanese art really exist solely to convey the artists' immersion in their own senses? Can they not be expected to make serious attempts to communicate with those who confront them and try to understand their true meaning? If we suppose that the senses here belong to the domain of taste, then Japanese art would have to be characterized as a solipsistic world wherein values were intuitive and spiritual. But if we consider it to be an expression of the collective unconscious of Japanese society, we will be able to find some objectively definable elements that run through the history of Japanese art.

Japanese art in its widest sense includes various disciplines that involve extensive training, such as the tea ceremony (*sadô*), flower arrangement (*kadô*), incense burning (*kôdô*) and calligraphy (*shodô*). These disciplines are each called a *dô* (way). In the non-artistic Japanese tradition, there are more *dô*, including swordsmanship (*kendô*), *jûdô*, and wrestling (*sumô-dô*). To attain the rank of an adept in these disciplines, one not only has to excel in them, but is also expected to have refined one's postures, techniques and movements based on one's own moral and aesthetic beliefs and everyday experiences. When a posture, a technique or a movement is refined to the ultimate, it becomes a *kata* (form). The accumulation of these *kata* is a *dô*. In that sense, a *dô* can be considered a body of aesthetics that has been distilled out of the collective unconscious.

Japanese jewellery of the 1990s enjoyed prosperity as a whole, though distinct artistic trends gradually disappeared from the scene. Perhaps we can consider that, in making this transition, jewellery design was turning into a *dô*. While Modernist influences were still felt, works that were based on 'purpose' and 'meaning' were considered significant, and this discouraged artists from displaying pieces that they felt would not be approved. But in the 1990s Modernist influences died down, and more importance came to be attached to forms and techniques, allowing this new type of work to come into its own.

An example of the new tendency can be found in the motifs of Mount Fuji and clouds with cranes employed by Keiko Sera. These are images she has rediscovered in Japanese tradition and adopted as her own. In the works of Ritsuko Ogura, we can see that, despite their seeming emphasis on concept, a traditional appreciation of paper texture plays an important role. Other artists are trying to reintroduce established patterns and textures into their works; an example is Ichiro Iino, who adopts the technique of *arashi-tsuchi* (roughing hammer) in his work.

Each of these artists makes use of traditional motifs or techniques in new ways, and still succeeds in creating works that can be readily accepted as contemporary pieces of jewellery. This kind of ingenious utilization of existing resources is enriching and widening the art form. So, Japanese jewellery is enjoying a renewed liveliness, though I have to admit that I did not expect the dwindling of cohesive and focused approaches to bring on a richer flowering.

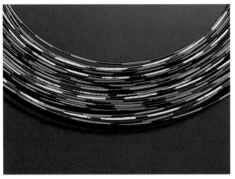

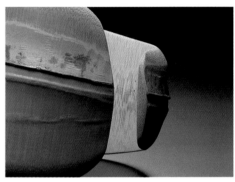

Aya Nakayama
Showzi Tsukamoto

Shinya Yamamura
Kimiaki Kageyama

Sakurako Matsushima
Tomomi Matsunaga

Jewellers in Focus

Of all the materials explored by jewellers in this catalogue, perhaps the most unusual is lacquer.

Lacquer's appeal is not only due to the longevity of its relationship with Japanese culture, but also because of its 'natural-ness', being derived from tree sap. After the sap has been processed, the consumer is left with a hyper-naturalistic object, wherein something natural is pushed technically to the point of artificiality.

The glossy depths of lacquer's shine cover a wide range of approaches to the material.

The work of **Aya Nakayama** is known in the West through her participation in international exhibitions. Using simple, often sculptural forms, she covers the surfaces of expanded foam, plastics and rattan with lacquer to make simple, wearable objects.

Showzi Tsukamoto combines lacquer with more traditional metal elements, creating jewellery that generates optical illusions, as the repeat elements, in motion, build up a rhythmic pattern.

The work of **Shinya Yamamura** is defined by the extraordinary quality of the lacquer work, luminous layers of coloured lacquers rubbed back to create contrasts. Two of the brooches illustrated here feature dense tufts of thick deer hair, the contrast between the glistening red surface and hair providing both abstract pattern and erotic charge. There is an underlying cruelty, too, in the languid coloured forms pierced by wires.

Kimiaki Kageyama's works are made from pieces of the lacquer carapace covering the surface of an ancient Kyoto shrine. The 300-year-old lacquer fragments, still curved and lustrous, define the shapes that they compose.

This recomposition creates a visual tension within the tactile objects that belies the simplicity of the concept.

Sakurako Matsushima has taken flight in the most dramatic way, making large, light, interlocking neckpieces in lacquer work. Comfortable to wear, they use a hemp-cloth base for the lacquer, a traditional armourer's technique, to deliver striking, dramatic body pieces. The refinement of both surface and form in her later pieces shows how her work has broken free of history to create its own area.

Only two makers featured here use bamboo, which is surprising given its myriad historical uses. **Tomomi Matsunaga** and **Chieko Shimizu** use the material in different ways for different purposes.

Matsunaga exploits the grain of the material and the large girth of some

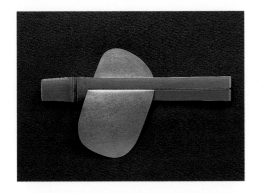

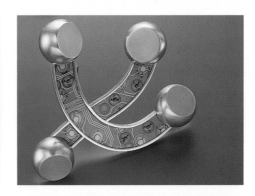
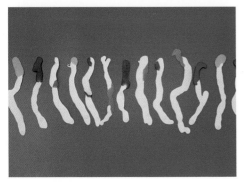

**Chieko Shimizu
Beniko Motonaga**

**Noriko Nagano
Mikiko Minewaki**

**Esmé Turid Yamaguchi
Yoshie Koba**

native varieties. This allows her to cut pieces from a single trunk, slicing in three dimensions to form torques and hairpieces.

Her most recent work is entirely different, exploiting the light flexibility of hemp cloth and the latest in contemporary metal pigments, providing flexible, light and wearable bracelets.

Shimizu creates work that is fixed to the body or clothing entirely by clips. This allows her to compose jewellery from an element of sheet gold and a piece of bamboo, the tensile qualities of the grass allowing her to create a clip-on object. Utilizing bamboo that is 100 years old and subtly stained by soot from a hearth brings a nostalgic quality to these spare elements.

Plastic is more rarely investigated in Japan than in Europe or the USA. **Beniko Motonaga**, who trained as a painter, brings painterly qualities and a fresh, open-minded clarity to her simple, short-life jewellery. She presents her pieces arranged on a coloured background, linking painting and wearability, and inviting you, in a sense, to paint your body.

Noriko Nagano works in both acrylic and in translucent industrial rubber. Her large, fluid pieces, composed by repetition, are intended to change constantly and move on the body. She has created a number of performances based around her work, collaborating with dancers, choreographers and lighting designers. The results allow her jewellery to occupy large architectural spaces.

Mikiko Minewaki approaches plastic differently, as she is part of a generation that connects through to Kazuhiro Itoh and the Three Schools Project. Devoted to her piercing saw, she excavates subtle bracelet and ring forms from traditional Japanese miso soup bowls, or rather from cheap plastic copies sold for everyday use, and from the plastic of the Bic lighters she and her friends use. The resulting jewellery comments on the values of one of the world's great consumer societies.

Esmé Turid Yamaguchi uses recycled pieces of plastic and circuit board in her explorations of consumer society, but frames them with silver to create large bold brooches and smaller vibrant pins, architectural in form, plastic replacing more traditional jewellery materials.

In a culture with a long history of using and creating specialist papers, it is no surprise to discover many jewellers featured here using it. A rich layer of values has accrued around the material, from its use in architecture to its rôle in the most intimate items.

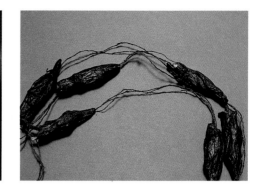
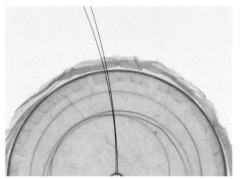

Kyoko Fukuchi
Eiji Suwa

Sae Yoshizawa
Kana Takenaka

Kyoko Urino
Ritsuko Ogura

The work of **Yoshie Koba**, with its twisted, delicate frameworks augmented with raku fired beads, has a strongly physical quality to it. Examination reveals its grey and black markings to have hidden qualities. The paper itself is antique, and the markings are brush-written kanji (Chinese characters); the sheets of paper are a series of old love letters, re-formed to rest comfortably around the neck. The reuse of paper echoes historical precedent, as it used to be recycled because of its great value.

The square, fragment forms of **Kyoko Fukuchi**'s work have brush-written script more directly inscribed on to their surfaces, with an overlay of tiny silver beads giving an almost Braille-like effect, enriching the surface of the *washi* (Japanese paper prized for its qualities).

Washi defines the work of **Eiji Suwa**. Presented as intended on a light box, the neckpiece elements – interchangeable translucent discs – allow the poetic qualities of *washi* and embedded elements to show, yet when worn combine to give controlled yet dramatic effects.

Sae Yoshizawa plays games with photographic images, catapulting them into form through the technique of origami. The results, accessible and playful, combine the wearability of fragments of sky or landscape with the strength of the repetitive folding, making rings that suggest a link between the wearer and the physical and metaphysical worlds.

Kana Takenaka uses the simplest paper-coiling techniques to form huge, swollen, oversize objects, which, recorded by home photography, provide a surreal quality, as if the jewellery is heavy visually but buoyant physically.

Kyoko Urino investigates the idea of natural materials in an artificial situation, partially copper-electroforming small branches to create uncertain identity and slicing them to fit the curve of the neck: part man-made, part truly natural.

Her most recent work has to do with wood, as paper, which is moulded into beads on a string and dyed with persimmon juice. Persimmon juice, long used as a staining agent in Japan, dyes the paper dark brown. The beads are deceptively light, the length of the necklace exactly matching that of Urino's own body.

The work of **Ritsuko Ogura** seeks to find beauty in a disregarded material. Both historically and through the teachings of Soetsu Yanagi, discovering beauty in a material of low value is a familiar approach in Japan. Ogura's modern twist is to use corrugated

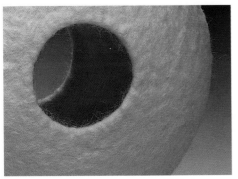

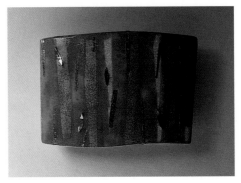

Masaki Yamamoto
Mikiko Aoki

Mayumi Matsuyama
Tomomi Arata   **Keiko Sera**

Haruko Sugawara
Hiroki Iwata

cardboard, painted then rolled up to provide a material to carve into. Hacking, carving, paring down, she uses a variety of cutting styles to find different expressions from a single starting point. The resultant chunky pieces, painted or charred, have an intense woody quality but are almost weightless to wear.

Textiles are represented in the catalogue by the work of **Masaki Yamamoto**, who trained as a textile artist and creates delicate woven fragments of intense colour. Furnished with pins, these pieces refer to the poetics of decay and Japan's textile history. Some, simply suspended, hang around the neck, but all have resonance as jewellery.

Mikiko Aoki is a self-taught jeweller who has created a collection from felted wool fibres. The large, round, white bracelet is soft and light to wear, but only accommodates one dent in its surface at

a time. A second dent and the tensile strength of the wool 'pops out' the original deformation.

Leather is also part of textile history, and the jewellery of **Mayumi Matsuyama** exploits her knowledge of the manufacture of leather goods, as she layers and bonds saw-edged leather pieces into bracelets. The structures' aggressive impact is tempered in wear by the nature of the materials.

Enamel work is a skill with a history connected to armour and costume. Enamelling is still practised and the four enamellers featured here use it to create very different personal statements.

Tomomi Arata's rings quite consciously have the air of having been excavated as sunken treasure. The enamel, mixed with sand, is fired on to rough-cast rings, then set with stones and, more recently, pearls.

She exploits the fragility of the mixture as the informal encrustations do not always remain, allowing the substructure of the ring to reappear.

Keiko Sera works with a very self-conscious 'Japaneseness', exploiting imagery that is both Japanese and kitsch. The grandeur of these images, when recreated in *cloisonné* enamel's bright, intense colours, imposes a childlike quality, reinforced by fabric elements and tassels. Her work is a product of, rather more than a commentary on, her native culture.

Haruko Sugawara uses enamel in quite a different way, burying structures of fine wire in enamel so that it fuses into glass. The resultant sculptural objects are visually strong and wearable, like fine drawings emerging from ice.

Hiroki Iwata is only at the beginning of his career, although his enamel work has

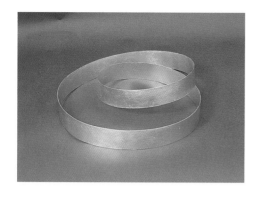
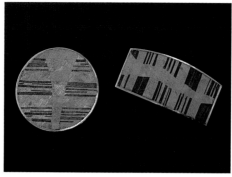

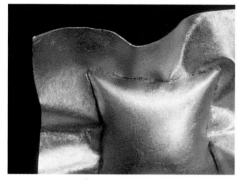
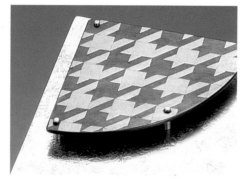
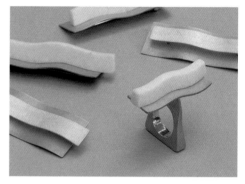

Yasuki Hiramatsu
Kozo Hiramatsu

Kaoru Nakano
Nobuko Abe

Yasuko Arai
Ichiro Iino

a distinctive personal quality, of matt, glacé surfaces enriched with fragments of gold leaf. Using the same techniques on vessels has helped him create larger jewellery objects than is common with enamel.

Jewellers for whom the focus of practice is an appreciation of and an experimentation with metals and metal techniques flourish in Japan. There is still great expectation of the exercise of skill and its application to small objects for delight and enjoyment.

Within this expectation, some jewellers explore making particular techniques their own; others move across possibilities; and yet others use materials as a basis for exploration. Some work is clearly materials-driven, other conceptual in origination and execution.

Probably the best-known jeweller internationally is **Yasuki Hiramatsu**, responsible for a long dialogue with

jewellers all over the world, consistently interested in making, and teacher to large numbers of jewellers. Hiramatsu's material playfulness belies his very real abilities with metal. This work is characterized by an interest in metal as a simple form, realized by sheet or wire from which brooches or other items are formed. Understated and careful in its execution, his work's influence can be seen and is credited in the work of other jewellers, including that of his son Kozo Hiramatsu. Acknowledging his father's influence, **Kozo Hiramatsu** explores metal in his own way, the inflated metal forms of his work showing a spontaneity that metal rarely achieves. The smooth volume contrasts with the corrugated and pleated surface that is a result of the inflation process. Both father and son choose different metal for different purposes, using the material as a palette.

Kaoru Nakano also uses metals as a palette, creating patterns inspired by textiles and inlaying the unusual combination of lead, silver and gold. The result is a distinctive coloured surface more akin to painting.

Inlay is a technique that is also practised by **Nobuko Abe**, its crisp and clearly defined boundaries providing the basis of his graphic op-art pieces, their dog-toothed checks again suggesting textiles as an inspiration. Abe's pattern-making, however, can spiral off into space and three dimensions.

Yasuko Arai explores different combinations of metal to inlay graphically pictorial pieces. Drawing moving and running figures from the cityscape indelibly on to the surface of her rings and brooches, many in rapid motion, she provides energy and a suggestion of narrative interrupted or unknown.

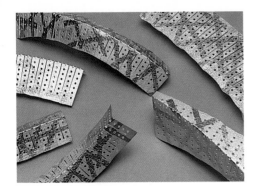
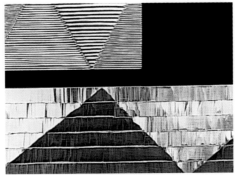
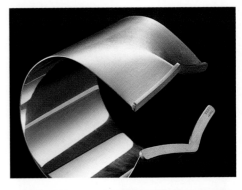
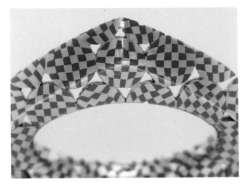

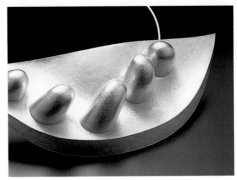

**Takashi Koyama
Yuta Hataya**

**Masafumi Sekine
Nagi Nakajima**

**Minato Nakamura
Mizuko Yamada**

Graphic qualities on metal surfaces are exploited in **Ichiro Iino**'s works, although he uses the ancient technique of mercury gilding to provide a soft, lustrous gold surface, inlaying colour combinations of gold, silver or platinum. The gentle geometry allows light to fall across carved surfaces of marble elements that share with the gilding similar characteristics of smoothness and lustre.

Although **Takashi Koyama**'s work is architecturally referenced and defined, the volumes punctured by small holes in a grid pattern, the pleasure of gold's lustre is no less important. Simply and crisply folded into brooches or light, bold chains, the punctured sheet metal conveys a discreet awareness of the interior of the volumes.

Yuta Hataya plays with the interiors of his subtle and wearable rings, using the early stages of a traditional metal technique, *mokumé gané*. He leaves fine triangular spaces among the soldered rods, visible only at the correct angle, when the apparently patterned surface suddenly reveals itself to be a collection of volumes forming the whole.

Surface is the key to the work of **Masafumi Sekine**, who uses a distinctive historical chisel technique to cut into the surface of the metal, creating a controlled brutality in the making of his marks. The metal has been cut away by the chisel's path to leave a glittering and dramatic surface that looks fresh and exciting. The simplicity of his work poses the question of how many techniques are really needed to create a piece of jewellery.

Nagi Nakajima uses a very different technique that reflects light equally well. She pleats and rolls sheet metal apparently as simply and easily as origami, which belies her craftsmanship.

Like a set of samples, only when worn on the body does the effectiveness of the work as jewellery become apparent.

The discipline learnt by Nakajima in the atelier of her teacher **Minato Nakamura** is very evident in Nakamura's own work. Her dexterity with silver and the quality of her surfaces contribute to the clear focus of her sculpturally informed work. Exploring ideas of the body in motion or at rest, she gives to her ring set a subtle human quality. Her most recent pieces, more explicitly sculptural, either fit close to the body or create a bold volume when sited on it.

Mizuko Yamada uses traditional metal-hammering techniques to create striking (huge in jewellery terms) volumes of metal, which have great presence in their own right. Unimaginable on the body, they have a scale and impact unusual for a Japanese artist and for metal jewellery in

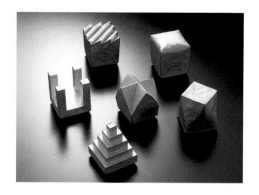

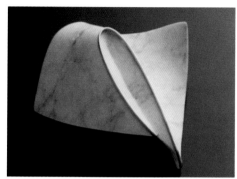

Toru Kaneko
Hiroko Sugiyama

Hiromasa Hashimoto
Emiko Suo

Masako Hayashibe

Reiko Yamada
Nobuko Nishiwaki

general. Worn, their strength is revealed; their weight seems regal rather than an imposition.

Toru Kaneko treats volume in a very different way, using simple cubic geometry in silver pieces that perch on the wearer, the three-dimensionality of the pieces enhanced by their soft surfaces.

Hiroko Sugiyama explores volumes through planes and lines around the fingers in particular, drawing in space with the metal to make small sculptural pieces that have a bold impact when worn.

Hiromasa Hashimoto uses geometric lines to make flexible sculptural pieces, the linking elements folding and pleating to make collars that can be bold or discreet according to the wearer's demands.

Also using line, in a very different way, is **Emiko Suo**. At home with wire multiples rather than sheet, Suo exploits the movement of fine rigid wires to create moving volumes of metal, sensitive to the slightest change of position in the wearer. The wires and filaments, recurrent elements in her work, are bound over forms in her latest pieces, giving an ambiguous depth to the surfaces of her bracelets.

The lines of **Masako Hayashibe**'s work are not metallic or rigid but are formed from silk and other textile threads, allowing for drape and fluidity, although strung with pearls and semi-precious stones. The composite bead pieces demonstrate the importance of repetition, as small elements build up into bigger objects.

Stones form an important element in the work of **Reiko Yamada**, who has been involved in making jewellery since the founding of the Japanese Jewellers Association. Her passions for the plasticity of gold and bold stones are matched, and in the pieces exhibited there is a tension between the volumes of stone and metal. Narrative and iconography also feature in her work.

Marble is the predominant material used in the pieces of **Nobuko Nishiwaki**, carved into forms reminiscent of folded paper or textile, the smooth crystalline surface of the material revealing its different qualities as the light hits the piece.

Qualities of light are expertly manipulated in the predominantly glass jewellery of **Kazuko Mitsushima**. Her twenty-five-year mastery of the possibilities of glass in jewellery and her manipulation of the jewellery form allow her to produce a wide variety of pieces. From experimental body and conceptual works to simple, wearable neckpieces, all

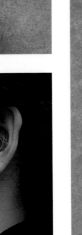

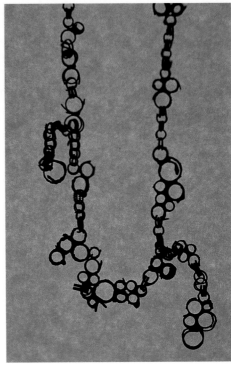

Teruo Akatsu
Hiroyuki Mashiko

Shinichiro Kobayashi
Masaki Takahashi

Ryuichiro Nakamura

exploit her understanding of the material. Embedding gold leaf or other elements inside the glass exploits the translucent qualities, and smashed fragments somehow suggest calligraphic imagery.

Lightness of a different form is captured in the dust pieces of **Teruo Akatsu**. Collecting dust from a variety of domestic environments, he exploits its transient nature, supporting his fragile surfaces with stainless-steel cores. Gold moulds in the form of rings allow other fragments of dust to coalesce into a felted ring of near-impossible wearability. Exploring meanings attracted to and accrued by jewellery, he also excavates jewellery from fragments of traditional clay roof tile, the structure of the tile defining by chance the final qualities of the neckpiece.

Hiroyuki Mashiko's materials have a function apart from that of making

jewellery. His neckpiece filled with lipstick would have a profound effect upon the wearer as the substance spread over the surfaces of the body and clothes: a cosmetic bloodbath.

Shinichiro Kobayashi also experiments with materials to help him create his works. He has made discoveries about the nature of ephemerality with his camphor-bead necklace, a necklace that disappears over time. The reverse is true of his kiss pieces, wherein the pressure of mouths kissing provides the master for a cast object, formed between two bodies and a physical act.

Masaki Takahashi takes an object (by Bernd Schobinger) from jewellery history about not hearing and punctures it to provide something for younger generations to wear that enables them to 'hear' and to listen, mixing wearability

and humour to change the meaning of a piece.

Ryuichiro Nakamura exploits the surroundings of the jewellery workshop rather than venturing out into the world: his work incorporates the remains of saw blades curled around into chains that cling to fabric and textile surfaces in gravity-defying ways. Other pieces are enriched with steel dressmaker's pins and tiny links of saw blades; all are beginning to rust.

Illustrated Biographies

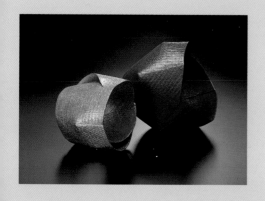

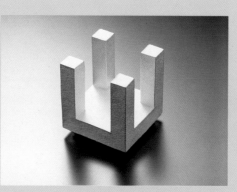

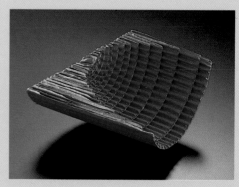

Irogane, brooch, 1998
6 × 6 × 1.5 cm
Silver 950, *shakudo*, copper, *hagiawase zougan*

I use *irogane* to produce jewellery. Used in Japan since ancient times, it is copper alloyed with a number of different metals that give different effects. The alloys I use are: *shakudo*, an alloy of copper and a small amount of pure gold which, when oxidized, gives a purplish-black colour; and *shibuichi* (literally meaning a quarter), which is an alloy of 75% copper to 25% silver, giving a grey oxidization. I also use pure copper, which oxidizes to a reddish-orange persimmon colour.

I use *irogane* alloys because they have colours all of their own, and I believe the colours of these alloys not to be inferior to those of precious metals and gems.

Nobuko Abe

Nobuko **Abe**

Nobuko Abe was born in Niigata in 1966. She studied jewellery design at the jewellery school in Akasaka, followed by a course in traditional Japanese metal techniques under Ichikawa Masami. Nobuko took part in group exhibitions of Japanese craft and jewellery art in 1997 and 1998. Her work is characterized by the use of a traditional ornamental inlay technique known as *nunome zougan*, or damascening.

Check on the Brooch, brooches, 1999
5.3 × 4.8 × 1.5 cm
6 × 4.3 × 1.5 cm
5.8 × 4.3 × 1.5 cm
Silver 950, *shakudo*, gold foil 999.9, *nunome zougan*

Illusion dust, brooches, 1993
Length 30 cm
Length 35 cm
Dust, stainless-steel wire, nickel silver

Teruo Akatsu was born in Tokyo in 1970, where he graduated from the Hiko Mizuno College of Jewellery in 1995. While still at college, he took part in several exhibitions, including *Jewelleryquake*, which toured Tokyo, Munich and Amsterdam, as well as *Japanese Contemporary Jewellery*, which was shown at the Museum of Decorative Arts in Ghent. Since then, his work has been included in group exhibitions in Japan and Germany.

Teruo **Akatsu**

I use fragments of roof tiles, which I cut up or carve. When worn on the body, the finished work appears to be an artificial form designed particularly for human use, and its functionality seems to be the main source of its beauty. However, it soon becomes clear how much of the work is the result of pure chance. It is not initially designed to ornament the body; its creation depends much more on the texture and shape of the material. With the paradoxical nature of my work, I hope to question the true meaning of jewellery.

I aim to transform 'negative' jewellery into positive existence by accumulating dust over it. The use of dust is suggestive of the passing and accumulation of time.

I collect dust from everyday places and thread it on to stainless-steel wires or incorporate it into sheets of material. The colours and nature of the dust play an important part in my jewellery-making.

The general conception of jewellery is focused on the fact that it adorns the body. However, this kind of understanding limits appreciation of my kind of jewellery. If we look at jewellery in terms of the relationship between the body and its surroundings, then we begin to see how we relate ourselves to objects, other people and our whole environment. With this in mind, the characteristics – including the advantages and disadvantages – of the materials themselves add meanings to my work.

Teruo Akatsu

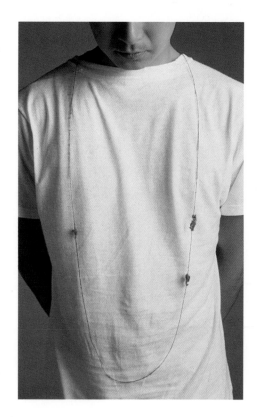

Illusion dust, necklace, 1993
35 × 35 cm
Dust, stainless-steel wire

Mikiko Aoki was born in 1948 in Shiga Prefecture. She studied industrial chemistry at Kyoto's Institute of Technology, graduating in 1983. The following year she was awarded first prize in the International Exhibition of Enamelling Art, Tokyo. Since then, her work has been included in numerous exhibitions around the world, notably the New York show *Artitudes* in 1989, *Jewellery Today Japan* in Trondheim, Norway, in 1991 and *Contemporary Japanese Craft and Jewelry Design* in Los Angeles in 1996.

Mikiko **Aoki**

Felted wool fibres allow me to produce large, hollow, three-dimensional works, which fold up neatly for storage, or can be pulled back into their original shapes. The work is light and soft, and dyeing allows me to use various colour schemes.
Mikiko Aoki

Bracelet, 1993
13 × 18 × 18 cm
Felted wool

A Moment, brooches, 1996
0.5 × 7.5 × 7.5 cm
0.5 × 7 × 7 cm
18k gold, 950 silver, *shakudo, kiribame zougan*

Yasuko Arai was born in Tokyo in 1945. She graduated from Musashino Art School with a degree in fine art in 1968, but has since pursued a career as a jeweller. Fascinated by the challenge of capturing the transitory nature of time and movement in her work, as well as taking part in group exhibitions in Japan, she has toured Norway with her jewellery and exhibited in galleries in Los Angeles and London. In 1984 Arai's work was acquired by the Schmuckmuseum Pforzheim, Germany, for its permanent collection.

Yasuko **Arai**

A Moment, rings, 1998
4.5 × 2.8 × 4 cm
5 × 2.8 × 4 cm
Silver, *niello* (alloy: gold, silver, lead and sulphur)

A Moment, rings, 1998
5.3 × 3 × 1.5 cm
5.3 × 3 × 1.5 cm
24k gold, 950 silver, *niello* (alloy: gold, silver, lead and sulphur)

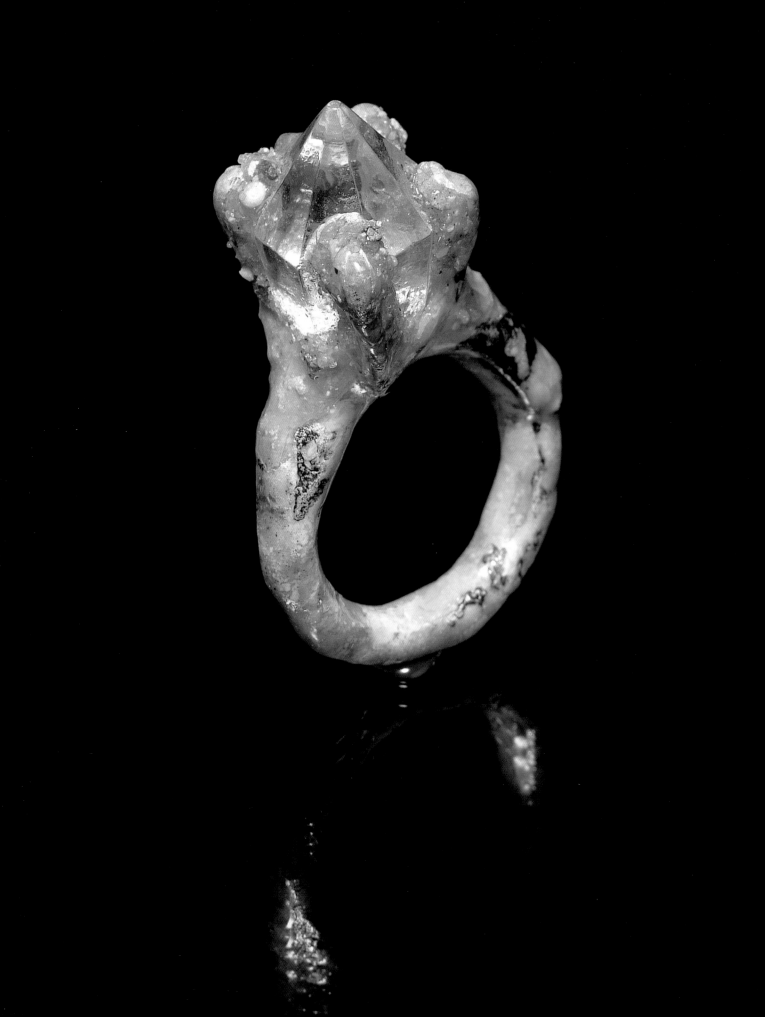

Treasures from Under the Sea, **ring 2, 1997**

3.8 × 2 × 1.5 cm

Hand-cast silver, enamel, glass, sand, purple stone

I am interested in change and the ways natural phenomena affect things – the erosion of objects on the beach, for example. I also often see shells, pebbles and sand clinging to rusty nails and cans on beaches.

I work with sand and enamel and I also use silver, which is the easiest of the precious metals to oxidize. I am intentionally trying to combine a man-made and a natural beauty.

Tomomi Arata

Tomomi **Arata**

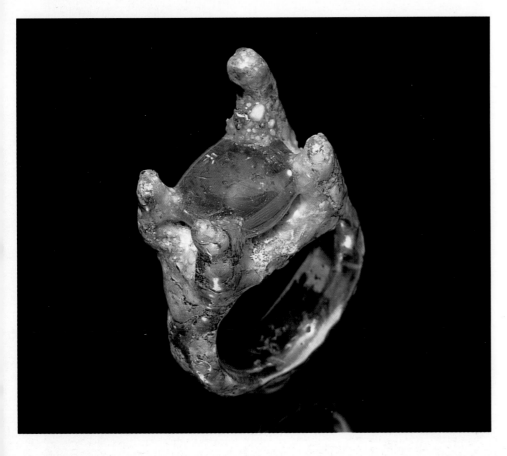

Tomomi Arata was born in 1967 in Kasama, Ibaragi Prefecture, and graduated from Hiko Mizuno College of Jewellery in Tokyo in 1990. The following year, she travelled to Amsterdam and enrolled at the Gerrit Rietvelt Academy, graduating in 1996. Despite returning to work in Japan, Arata has maintained strong links with Europe, exhibiting in Holland and Germany from 1996 to 1999.

Treasures from Under the Sea, **ring 1, 1997**

2.5 × 2 × 1 cm

Hand-cast silver, enamel, glass, sand, clear stone

Kyoko Fukuchi was born in 1946 in Hiroshima and studied at the Musashino Junior College of Fine Art in 1966. She has exhibited her work internationally: first touring Europe in 1983, she has since showed in Lausanne in 1989, in Paris in 1990 and in London in 1997. In 2000 her jewellery was included in *Ways of Working* and *Metals Studio Launch* at Monash University in Melbourne.

Echo of Time Past, brooch, 2000

4.8 × 5 × 3 cm

Hemp paper

Echo of Time Past, brooch, 2000
7.3 × 7.3 × 0.7 cm
Hemp paper

 Kyoko **Fukuchi**

I use *washi* paper from *daifukucho*, the old style of Japanese account books.
My family has been engaged in the drapery business for about 130 years. As writing
pens were not available in Japan in the nineteenth century, all necessary records were
made on *washi*, using a brush and indian ink. My great-grandfather wrote these words
in ink about 100 years ago. They are like memory flowing through my body.
The theme of my work is the scenery of my mind; I try to recall an echo of time past,
although it is not always feasible.
I aim to express in the form of jewellery what is intangible. For this, *washi*, which is a
soft and ambiguous material without the definite form and line of metal, is necessary.
In processing metals, fire, chisels, hammers and other tools are employed, and these
intervene between myself and the metals. However, my fingers are in direct contact with
the paper and my thoughts are transmitted directly into it. This is the essential difference.
Kyoko Fukuchi

Ruten, necklace, 1999
24 × 24 × 4 cm
Silver and silicone cord

Hiromasa Hashimoto was born in Tokyo in 1967 and graduated from the Kuwasawa Design Institute as an industrial designer in 1991. After five years working for an industrial design company, he enrolled at the Hiko Mizuno College of Jewellery in Tokyo, graduating in 1999. His preferred materials are silver and silicone cord, and in his series *Ruten* he explores the concept of repeat patterns.

Hiromasa **Hashimoto**

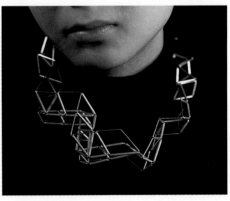

Ruten, necklace, 1999
24 × 24 × 4 cm
Silver, silicone cord

Ruten, necklace, 1999
24 × 24 × 4 cm
Silver, silicone cord

Yuta Hataya was born in Tokyo in 1977 and has studied extensively at the Hiko Mizuno College of Jewellery, first completing a jewellery design product course in 1999 and continuing with the school's advanced programme, graduating in 2000. His work – characterized by the interplay of two metals, copper alloy and silver – was included in the International Craft Exhibition at the Museum of Crafts in Itami in 1999 and the 21st Japan Jewellery Exhibition, Tokyo, in 2000.

Yuta **Hataya**

Metal Fibre, ring, 1999
2.8 × 2.3 × 0.4 cm
Silver, copper

Metal Fibre, ring, 1999
2.8 × 2.3 × 0.4 cm
Silver, copper

Metal Fibre, ring, 1999
2.7 × 2.3 × 0.4 cm
Silver, *kuromido*

Rhizome (neckware I and II), 1998

4 × 14 × 2 cm

Diameter 13 cm

Glass beads, fishing thread

When I was an exchange student in a high school in the USA, I was given a silver dollar ring that had been flattened on the tram tracks – this later became illegal. At that time, Japan was suffering the aftermath of the Second World War, and nobody cared for silver or for jewellery. I came to know the beauty and preciousness of this white metal then. The intention of my work is to give the wearer freedom. My objects are subject to the wearer's physical shape, and it is up to him or her to decide where and how they want to wear my pieces.

I am now interested in more ephemeral materials such as flimsy Japanese paper. My intention is that the pieces will belong to the wearer for a certain period of time and then return to nature in a relatively short time, as we corporeal human beings shall. We will be able to watch the beauty of decay as well.

Masako Hayashibe

Masako **Hayashibe**

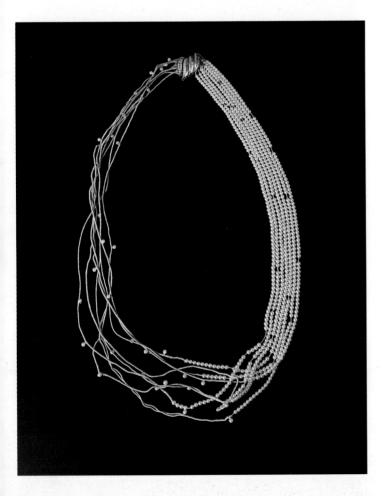

Masako Hayashibe was born in Tokyo in 1940. She studied German at Tokyo University of Foreign Studies, graduating in 1965, before spending a year in Sweden, where she studied religious history and textiles in Stockholm. The influence of textiles is apparent in many of the techniques – such as crochet and weaving – that Masako explores in her jewellery. Her work has been exhibited at numerous group and solo exhibitions since 1986, when she won the grand prix at the Asahi Modern Craft Exhibition in Tokyo and Osaka.

A River Flows, necklace, 1994

72 cm

Silk, pearls, platinum

Kozo Hiramatsu was born in Osaka in 1953. He did not finish his college education, but trained under his father, Yasuki Hiramatsu. Since 1988 he has had numerous solo exhibitions in Japan and has taken part in several group shows in Belgium and Germany, including the international jewellery exhibition *Schmuck* in Munich, where his work has appeared twice: in 1997 and in 1999. He has won several awards, including the 'Excellence' prize at the 1989 Japanese Craft Exhibition, Tokyo, and second prize at *Signaturen*, the international jewellery competition held in Schwäbisch Gmünd, Germany.

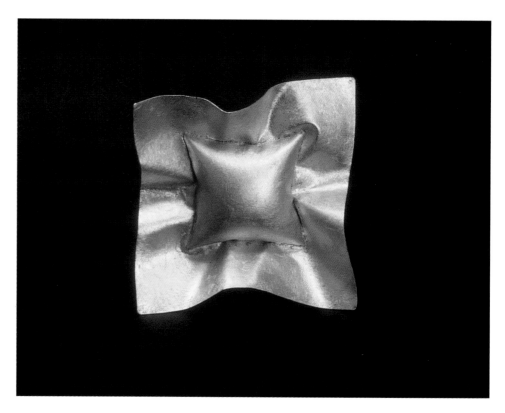

***Expansion*, brooch, 2000**
13 × 13 × 5 cm
Copper, gold leaf

My design takes form while I am actually working on materials. Rather than producing my work by strictly following an initial pattern, I tend to create things through the impact I make on my materials, reacting to the responses returned from them. This kind of method, I believe, shows my father's influence on me.

I avoid using gold or platinum (although I use them elsewhere) when creating suggestive or expressive works, as these materials, and precious stones, tend to be valued merely for their worth as materials. I see this as disadvantageous when creating a work.

Kozo Hiramatsu

Kozo **Hiramatsu**

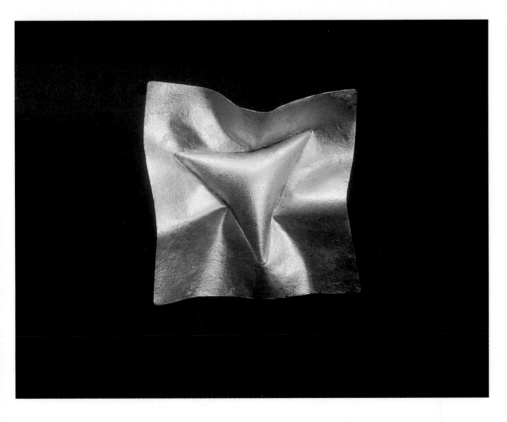

***Expansion*, brooch, 2000**
13.5 × 13 × 3.5 cm
Copper, gold leaf

Necklace, 1999

27 × 27 × 10 cm

950 silver and gold plate

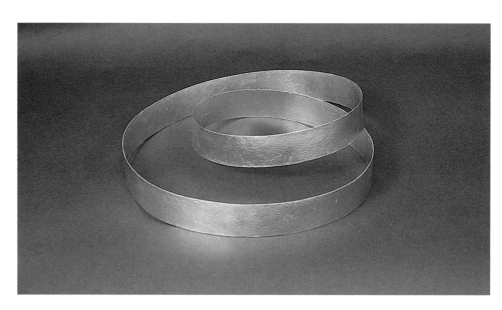

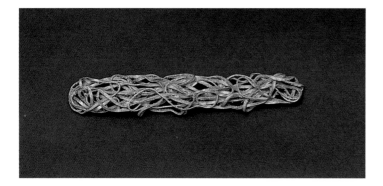

Brooch, 1999

14.9 × 2.5 × 1.6 cm

950 silver and gold plate, gold leaf

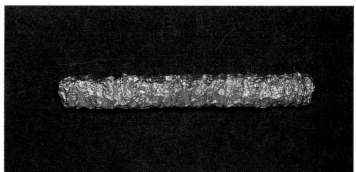

Brooch K22, 2000

1.8 × 13.3 × 1.1 cm

Silver, gilding

Yasuki Hiramatsu was born in Osaka in 1926. In 1952 he graduated from the Tokyo National University of Fine Arts and Music, where he is now president. He has received several awards in public recognition of his work, including the 41st Crafts Award in Excellence (1991), awarded by the Japanese Ministry of Education, and the award for Contribution to Design Promotion (1995), awarded by the Japanese Ministry of Trade and Industry, and has taken part in numerous group and solo exhibitions around the world. His jewellery is held in several public collections, including those of the Royal College of Art and the Victoria and Albert Museum in London.

Yasuki **Hiramatsu**

Necklace, 1999
27 × 27 × 10 cm
Aluminium, gold leaf

Brooch K20, 1998
5.6 × 5.4 × 2.5 cm
Gilding

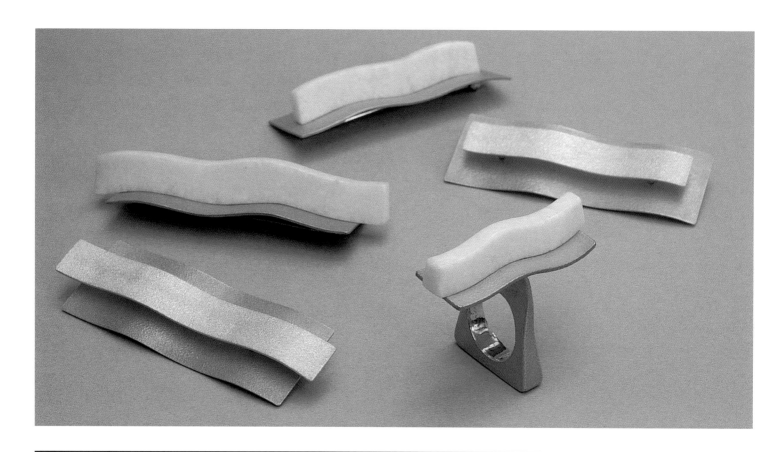

Ichiro **Iino**

Ichiro Iino was born in 1949 in Saitama Prefecture. In 1975 he graduated in metal carving from the Tokyo National University of Fine Arts and Music. In 1998 he was appointed Director of the Japan Jewellery Designers Association, and, over the years, he has taken part in numerous group and solo exhibitions around the world. His work has been collected by Tokyo University Art Museum, Tokyo National Modern Art Museum and Toyodacho Fragrance Museum.

Brooches, 1997
Ring, 1997
8.3 × 2.5 × 1 cm
7.2 × 2.6 × 1.5 cm
8.5 × 2.6 × 1.7 cm
4.5 × 2.7 × 4 cm (ring)
Silver, amalgam, gilding, marble

Brooch, 1999
7.6 × 2.3 × 0.85 cm
Silver, Pt 900, amalgam, gilding

Hiroki Iwata was born in Tokyo in 1965 and studied applied arts at the Tokyo National University of Fine Arts and Music, graduating in 1990. Two years later he returned there to take a master's degree in metal carving. Since 1991 his work has been exhibited in Japan and Germany, and he has won several awards, notably for his trademark use of enamel.

Hiroki **Iwata**

Antiquity, brooch, 1999
4.5 × 6.5 × 0.8 cm
Silver, enamel, 18k gold, gold foil, silver leaf

Black, brooch, 1999
6 × 4.5 × 0.8 cm
Silver, enamel, gold foil, gold leaf

Green, brooch, 1999
White, necklace, 1999
2 × 12 × 0.9 cm
9.5 × 3.5 × 1 cm
Silver, enamel, silver foil, silver leaf
Silver, enamel, 18k gold, silver foil

Kimiaki Kageyama was born in Sizuoka in 1948 and studied metalwork at the Tokyo National University of Fine Arts and Music, completing a BA in 1972 and an MA in 1974. His work has been exhibited widely in Tokyo, both in solo and group shows, and in 1992 he took part in *Contemporary Japanese Jewellery* at the Electrum Gallery in London. He was awarded the 'Superior' prize at the 1980 Japanese Craft Exhibition, Tokyo, and the Tansui-oh Award at the Satoh Foundation, Tokyo, in 1989.

The Heart, brooch, 2001
Suzushita, brooch, 2001
1.5 × 6.8 × 9.3 cm
2 × 4 × 9 cm
Urushi, hemp, resin, mineral pigments (black),
gold paint

The Heart, brooch, 2001
1.5 × 6.8 × 9.3 cm
Urushi, hemp, resin, mineral pigments (black),
gold paint

I aim to observe everyday life in Japan and find materials and methods that will encourage us to question its modernity and social meanings. The fragments of portable shrine were crafted by worker–craftsmen during the Edo period 300 years ago; now piled up in a bin bag about to be thrown away, they are merely discarded waste. Viewed from another angle, they provide unexpectedly innovative materials for jewellery alluding to the question of modernity.

Kimiaki Kageyama

Suzushita, **brooch, 2001**
2 × 4 × 9 cm
Urushi, hemp, resin, mineral pigments (black),
gold paint

Kimiaki **Kageyama**

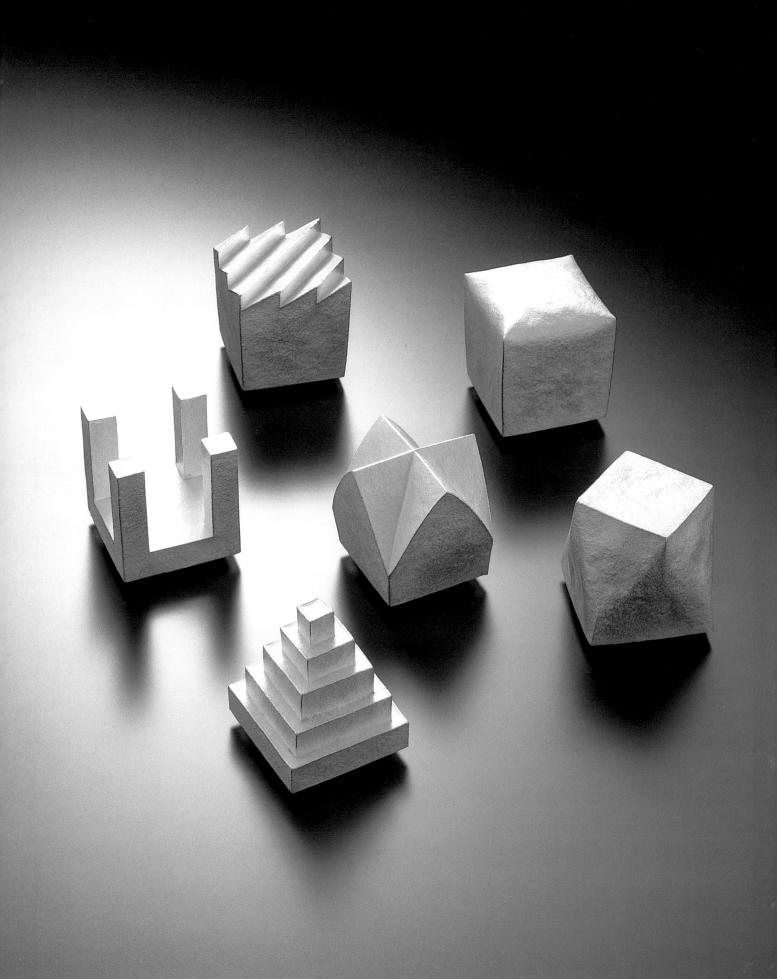

Shoulder brooches, 1994

5 × 4.5 × 4.5 cm

Silver

Toru Kaneko was born in Tokyo in 1962
and studied silversmithing at the Tokyo
National University of Fine Arts and Music,
graduating in 1988. He has been awarded
several prizes for his jewellery: first in
1993 at the exhibition *The Art of Jewellery*,
Tokyo, again in 1996 at the Japanese Craft
Exhibition, Tokyo, and in 1997 at the
Takaoka Craft Exhibition, Toyama, Tokyo.
Kaneko is now a lecturer in metal art at
Tohoku University of Art and Design.

Toru **Kaneko**

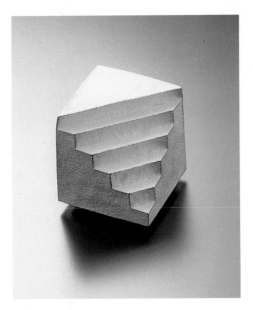

Shoulder brooch, 1994

5 × 4.5 × 4.5 cm

Silver

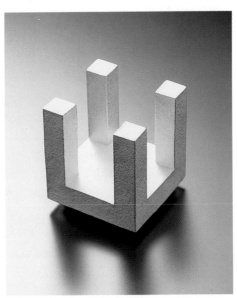

Shoulder brooch 2, 1994

5 × 4.5 × 4.5 cm

Silver

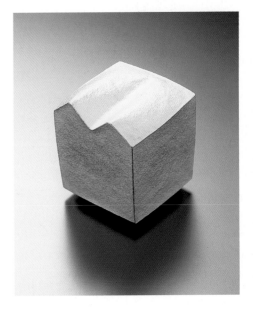

Shoulder brooch 9, 1994

5 × 4.5 × 4.5 cm

Silver

Necklace, 1998
25 × 20 × 5 cm
Traditional Japanese paper, bisque fired

Time fading away, brooch, 1994
22 × 17 × 8 cm
Traditional Japanese paper, bisque fired

Yoshie Koba was born in Kobe in 1942, where she still lives and works. First attracted to sculpture when she worked as an apprentice in a sculptor's studio, she began to explore how to make jewellery. Self-taught, she predominantly uses silver juxtaposed with traditional Japanese handmade papers. In 1993 she was awarded a prize in the Japan Jewellery Designers Association jewellery contest in Japan, and in 1997 her work was exhibited at the Lesley Craze Gallery in London.

Yoshie **Koba**

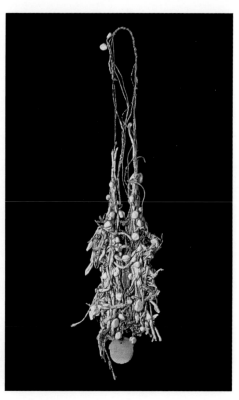

Time fading away, necklace, 1993
110 × 40 × 10 cm
Traditional Japanese paper, bisque fired

Time fading away, necklace, 1994
130 × 20 × 5 cm
Traditional Japanese paper, bisque fired

Shinichiro Kobayashi was born in 1969 in Shizuoka. He graduated from the Hiko Mizuno College of Jewellery in Tokyo in 1993. His jewellery, which is characterized by a unique juxtaposition of precious metals and charcoal, has been widely exhibited in Tokyo and Europe since 1991. In 1993 he took part in *Jewelleryquake*, an exhibition that toured Tokyo, Munich and Amsterdam, and in 1997 his work was included in *Schmuck*, the international jewellery show held in Munich.

White Dew, **necklace, 1994**
32 × 15 × 2 cm
Camphor, stainless-steel wire

Point of Contact **(detail), 1993**
3 × 2 × 2 cm
Cast gold

Shinichiro **Kobayashi**

I aim to surprise my audience with an innovative choice and use of materials. For example, camphor, after I have transformed it from insect repellent into jewellery, melts and re-shapes itself as time goes by, releasing its characteristic smell. I see a special quality of existence in this process.

Shinichiro Kobayashi

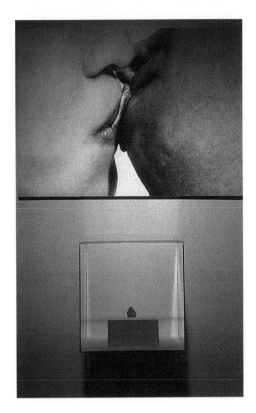

Point of Contact, 1993
100 × 60 × 30 cm
Photograph and boxed, pure, cast gold

Necklaces, 1998
3.5 × 23 cm diameter
Silver, platinum
Silver, gold

Takashi Koyama was born in Tokyo in 1967. He graduated from the Hiko Mizuno College of Jewellery in 1987, where he stayed to complete a product-research training programme, winning a prize at his graduation in 1990. His work, which is predominantly in silver and gold, has been selected for several group crafts and jewellery art exhibitions in Japan.

Takashi **Koyama**

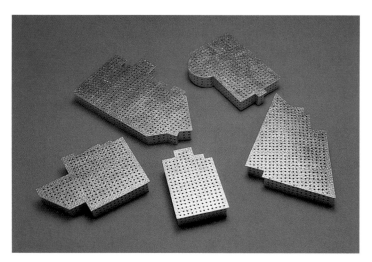

An Apartment, **brooches, 1999**
6.5 × 4.7 × 1.1 cm
9.1 × 5.6 × 1.1 cm
5.1 × 3.3 × 1.1 cm
4.9 × 6.6 × 1.1 cm
8.8 × 5.5 × 1.1 cm
Silver, gold

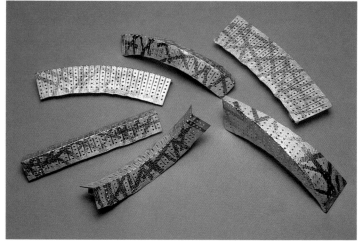

Brooches, 1995
2.4 × 9.5 × 1 cm
2.4 × 9.9 × 1.2 cm
2 × 9 × 1.3 cm
2 × 9.6 × 1.2 cm
2 × 9.5 × 1.2 cm
Silver, gold

Hiroyuki Mashiko was born in Tochigo Prefecture in 1960. He graduated from the Hiko Mizuno College of Jewellery in 1989, but stayed on to work there as a lecturer until 2000. His work, which has been included in numerous group exhibitions both in Japan and Europe, makes use of such surprising materials as plastic toys, sandpaper and human hair.

Hiroyuki **Mashiko**

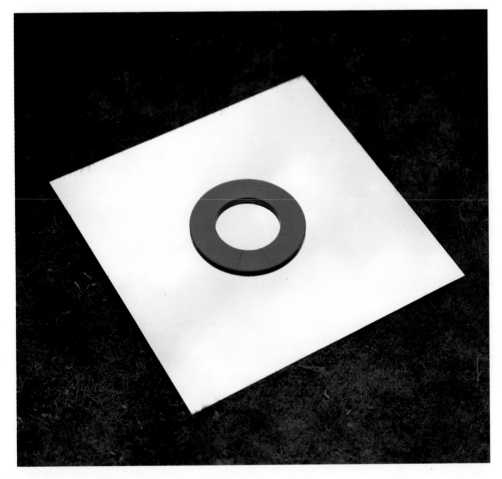

I don't use specific materials and methods. I view jewellery as more than simply ornamentation, but rather as an expression of the relationship between my work, society and myself. My creations reflect this tripartite relationship. I believe that as long as one remains involved with oneself as a human being, one need not confine oneself to specific materials and methods.
Hiroyuki Mashiko

Rouge, necklace, 1994
1.2 × 36 × 36 cm
Carmine, 950 silver, chromium plate

67

Mitsuo Masuda was born in Saitama Prefecture in 1909. He studied metal carving at the Tokyo National University of Fine Arts and Music and graduated in 1936. Over the years he has taken part in numerous group and solo exhibitions, and his work was featured at the *Craft Masterwork Living National Treasure* exhibition at Urawa Art Museum in 2000. In recognition of his cultural contribution he has received many awards, notably the Medal of Purple Ribbon (1976) and the Order of the Sacred Treasure (1982), while in 1991 he was named an Important Intangible Cultural Property. His work now forms part of the permanent collection held by the Japanese Ministry of Foreign Affairs.

Brooch

7.3 × 4.5 × 1 cm

Silver, gold, ruby, chasing, *katakiri* carving, mercury gilding

Ring
2 × 1.5 × 2.4 cm
Silver, chasing, soldering

Mitsuo **Masuda**

Ring
2.4 × 1.5 × 3 cm
Silver, garnet, filing, soldering

Tomomi Matsunaga was born in Kyoto in 1954 and graduated from Saga Junior College of Art in 1975. Her work is characterized by the use of carved bamboo, which she coats with a traditional Japanese lacquer finish. Since graduation, she has been selected to take part in several craft exhibitions and competitions throughout Japan. In 1986 her work was included in the show *Bamboo Artwear* in Los Angeles, and in 1999 she took part in *Ikebana and Art Work* at the Museum Rietberg in Zürich.

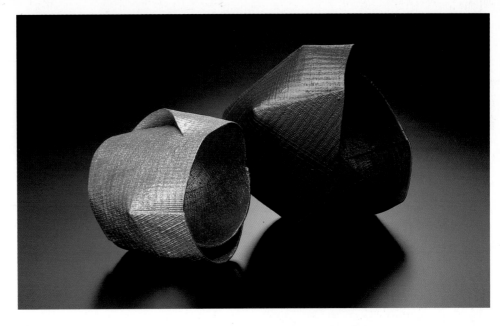

Natural bamboo necklace, 2001
8 × 15 × 24 cm
Bamboo

Silver Coil, bracelet, 2001
Beni (carmine), bracelet, 2001
6.5 × 6 × 4.5 cm
7 × 9 × 7 cm
Linen, metal-leaf paint

Tomomi **Matsunaga**

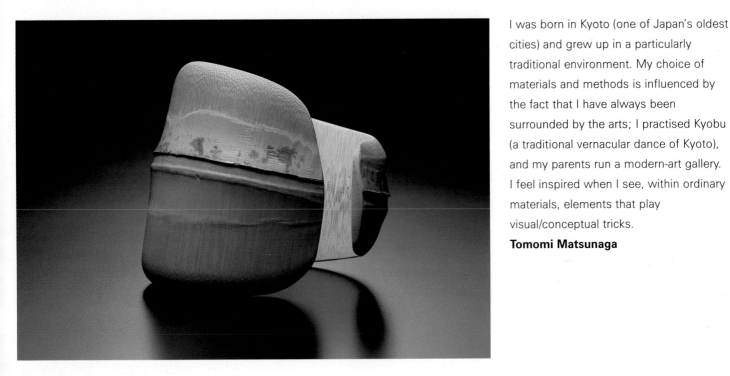

I was born in Kyoto (one of Japan's oldest cities) and grew up in a particularly traditional environment. My choice of materials and methods is influenced by the fact that I have always been surrounded by the arts; I practised Kyobu (a traditional vernacular dance of Kyoto), and my parents run a modern-art gallery. I feel inspired when I see, within ordinary materials, elements that play visual/conceptual tricks.

Tomomi Matsunaga

Natural bamboo bracelet, 2001
7.5 × 8 cm
Bamboo

Sakurako Matsushima was born in Tokyo in 1965. She studied lacquer work at the Tokyo National University of Fine Arts and Music, graduating in 1991, before undertaking a further year of research in the metal jewellery department. In 1997 she completed a second research programme into the history of Chinese art and craft at the Central Academy of Arts and Design, Beijing. Her work has been widely exhibited internationally and is included in several publications about lacquer work.

Upper-body ornament, 2000
64 × 53 × 10 cm
Urushi, hemp cloth, Mexican abalone, mother-of-pearl, gold powder, leather

Necklace, 2000
26 × 24 × 1.5 cm
Urushi, eucalyptus leaves, hemp cloth, Mexican abalone, gold powder, tin powder

Sakurako **Matsushima**

Breast ornament, 2000
44 × 24 × 5.5 cm
Urushi, hemp cloth, Mexican abalone, gold powder, tin powder

I have always made body ornamentation. At first I made jewellery for myself and only for myself. Then I began asking myself, Why do we humans ornament ourselves? In Japan, lacquer jewellery has been found from as far back as 6000 years ago. At its root, body ornamentation is spiritual. It was – and is – worn at religious rites and rites of passage; it marks which group one belongs to and one's place in the group. I began to study ancient *urushi* and its use in body ornamentation, as well as other lacquer cultures and the uses of *urushi* by the peoples of Asia. I wanted to know why these ornaments were and are being made, and what connection *urushi* has with the spiritual in their and our lives. In my work I want to express other aspects of human existence – to bring out the spiritual dimension within.
Sakurako Matsushima

Bracelets, 1996

7 × 22 × 22 cm

Leather

Mayumi Matsuyama was born in Osaka in 1951 and now lives and works in Kyoto. She first began to explore jewellery at Mukogawa Junior College, where she studied art and interior design, graduating in 1971. Her work, which combines leather with silver and brass, has been included in several solo and group craft exhibitions throughout Japan.

Mayumi **Matsuyama**

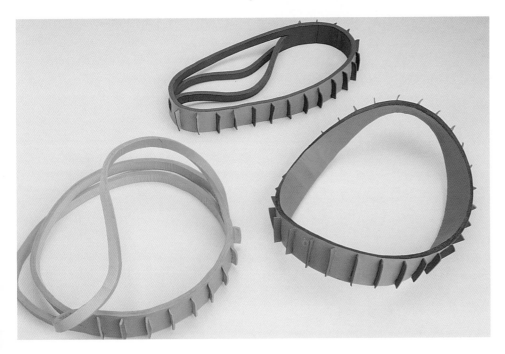

Caterpillar, necklaces, 1999
4.5 × 32 × 32 cm
Leather

One de wan, ring, 1999
1 × 2.8 × 3 cm
Miso soup bowl

One de wan, ring and bracelet series, 1999
1 × 2.8 × 3 cm
2 × 7 × 6 cm
Miso soup bowl

Mikiko Minewaki was born in Akita Prefecture in 1967. Today she lives in Kanagawa Prefecture and works in Tokyo, having studied at the Hiko Mizuno College of Jewellery, where she is now a lecturer. Her work, which makes use of brightly coloured plastic products that remind her of her childhood, has toured Europe in both group and solo exhibitions, including the international craft show *Schmuck* in Munich in 1999. Several galleries in Belgium and Germany have acquired her jewellery for their permanent collections.

Sugarcoated Yellows:
Pla-rings and One de wan rings, 2000
3 × 2.5 × 1 cm
Disposable lighters, miso soup bowls

Pla-ring, 2000
3 × 2.5 × 1 cm
Disposable lighter

I was born in the countryside in Japan. Every day I picked flowers and leaves from the fields and made jewellery – necklaces, rings, crowns – from them. This is the source of my making.
One day I found that these natural forms were hidden in plastic products. So I started to pick a selection of them from my daily objects, and I am now searching for new forms in my day-to-day objects.
Mikiko Minewaki

Mikiko **Minewaki**

Ring, 1998
3 × 3 × 1.8 cm
Glass, silver

Ring, 1998
5 × 3 × 2.8 cm
Glass, 18k gold

Kazuko Mitsushima was born in 1946 in Hyogo Prefecture. She studied psychology at Konan University and graduated in 1969. Her work has been widely exhibited, both in group and in solo shows internationally. Characterized by a delicate use of glass, Mitsushima's award-winning jewellery is included in the permanent collections of the Hiko Mizuno College of Jewellery in Tokyo, the Corning Museum of Glass in New York and the National Museums of Scotland in Edinburgh.

Kazuko **Mitsushima**

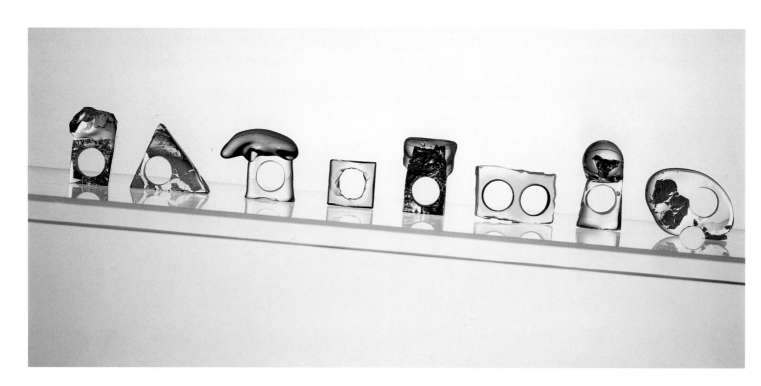

Rings, 1993
3 x 5 x 1 cm approximately
Blown glass

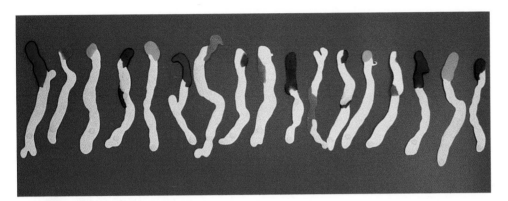

Colours, **1999**
57 × 99 cm
Resin

Beniko **Motonaga**

Beniko Motonaga was born in Hyogo in 1968 and graduated from Osaka Art University in 1991. She has been invited to take part in several group exhibitions in Japan since 1997, including the Asahi Modern Craft Exhibition in Osaka and Tokyo in 1997 and 1998, and the International Craft Exhibition at the Museum of Crafts in Itami in 1999, where she was awarded the 'Good Material' prize. Motonaga has also held two solo exhibitions in Kyoto, first at the Gallery Maronie in 1999, and then at the Gion Konishi Gallery in 2000.

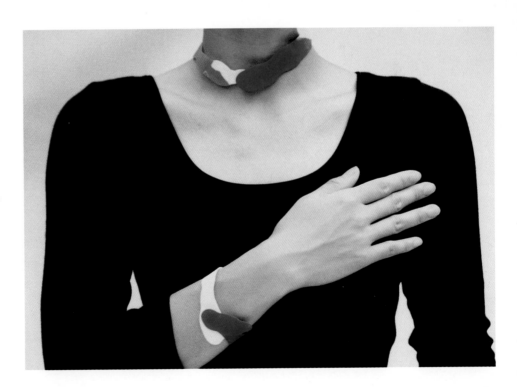

Colours, **1999**
57 × 99 cm
Resin

Neckpiece II, 1996
60 × 60 × 0.5 cm
Urethane rubber

Noriko Nagano was born in Tokyo in 1941 and graduated from Joshibi Art University in Tokyo in 1962. She has taken part in several group exhibitions in Japan, including the series of shows *Element*, a collaboration with dance, music and photography, beginning in 1994 and continuing in 1997. For this series, Noriko published an album, for which she received the Best Poster and Catalogue award from the Printing and Publishing Institute, Tokyo, in 1994. Her work is characterized by the use of acrylic and urethane rubber.

The works I make in acrylic and rubber do not stay fixed but transform themselves depending on how they are worn and how a body moves in them. I am interested in new materials and new processes and how to make the best use of such materials. I collaborate with artists from different fields: dancers, musicians, lighting designers and so on. I find I draw most inspiration from the creative processes of the pieces I make and from my collaborative works with other people.
Noriko Nagano

Noriko **Nagano**

Neckpiece I, 1994
110 × 10 × 3 cm
Urethane rubber

Spiral, **brooch, 2000**
2 cm diameter × 30 cm long
Silver

Spiral, **brooches, 2000**
2 cm diameter × 30 cm long
2.5 × 2.5 × 23 cm
4 × 13 × 7 cm
Silver

Nagi Nakajima was born in Tokyo in 1967. She graduated from Tama Art University in 1989 and has taken part in several jewellery, metalwork and craft exhibitions in Japan and Germany. In 1999 she was awarded a prize at the Asahi Modern Craft Exhibition in Osaka and Tokyo and won third prize at the international jewellery competition *For You – For Me* in Gmünd, Germany. In 2000 she was awarded first prize at the Japanese Jewellery Art Competition, Tokyo.

Nagi **Nakajima**

Ori-Kite, brooch, 1998
3 × 9 × 8.5 cm
Silver

Ori-Spiral, bangles, 1999
3.5 × 7 × 6.5 cm
Silver, gold

I like to think of my pieces as wearable art objects. The advantage of working with silver is that out of all the precious metals it is the most lightweight and elegant and it allows me to express space and shape.
Nagi Nakajima

Out of Joint, rings, 1994
5.5 × 3.2 × 2 cm approximately
The National Museum of Modern Art, Tokyo
Silver

Minato Nakamura was born in Tokyo in 1947. She studied sculpture at the Musashino Art University and graduated in 1969 before going on to explore jewellery making. She has exhibited internationally: at the 19th International Jewellery Exhibition in Serge, Yugoslavia (1985) where she was awarded silver prize, at *Schmuck* (1989) in Munich, in Belgium (1995), Denmark (1996) and Australia (1999). Her work is held in several public collections in both Kyoto and Tokyo.

Bracelet, 1999
5 × 6 × 5.5 cm
Silver

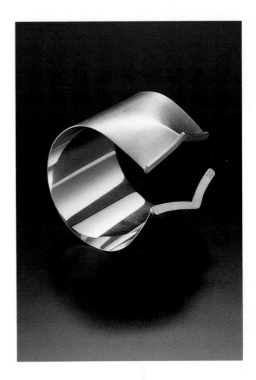

Minato **Nakamura**

I love silver. I want to show the warmth and gentleness of metals, and I feel this especially in silver. I have been making silver jewellery for a long time, and so silver feels like an old friend. As I dislike tormenting the material, I follow its nature, using simple methods.

The colour of silver changes with time. I think this is an advantage because time is therefore incorporated into my work. When, for example, I am on a train, I get ideas for my work, as most of my inspiration comes from watching people's bodies and movements in various situations.

Minato Nakamura

Brooch, 1999
4 × 8.4 × 6 cm
Silver

I have developed a jewellery based on the theme of thorns over the past ten years. The nature of thorns does not allow them to fit into the general conception of jewellery; however, it is possible for them to ornament the body, and 'thorn jewellery' has a special appeal for me. I used to concentrate on silver as my chosen medium, but for the past five or six years I have mainly been using iron sheet, hammered or curved.

Now I make use of anything I can: broken tips of saws and metal tools, parts of machinery and empty cans.

I personally believe that jewellery does not consist only of sparkling, light, easy-to-wear pieces, just as human beings, the world and its history contain diverse and incompatible elements.

Ryuichiro Nakamura

Ryuichiro **Nakamura**

Ryuichiro Nakamura was born in Tokyo in 1969. He studied at the Hiko Mizuno College of Jewellery, graduating in 1994, and has remained involved with the contemporary jewellery course, working first as an assistant in 1995, and since 1999 as a part-time teacher. He has taken part in several group exhibitions in Japan, Finland and Belgium, and in 1999 held a solo exhibition in Tokyo.

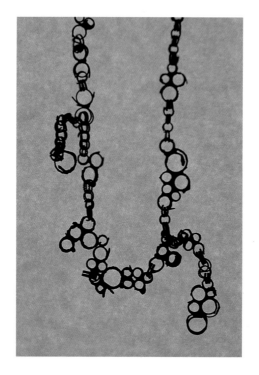

Unforgettable Shine, necklace, 2001
42 × 52 × 7 cm boxed
Saw blade, pins, specimen box

Unforgettable Shine, necklace, 1999
40 cm
Saw blade

The quiet silence III and IV, brooches, 1997
6 × 6 × 0.1 cm
3.5 × 7 × 0.1 cm
Silver, gold leaf, lead leaf, inlaid work

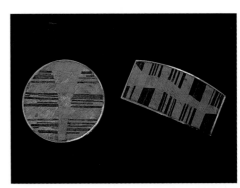

Kaoru **Nakano**

Kaoru Nakano was born in Shiga in 1949 and studied literature at Ryukoku University, Kyoto, graduating in 1972. She now lives and works in Hiroshima. Her jewellery has been included in several group exhibitions in Japan since 1995, including the Takaoka Craft Exhibition in Toyama, Tokyo (1995), Jewellery Art Competition, Tokyo (1996), Japanese Craft Exhibition, Tokyo (1996–99), International Craft Exhibition, Itami (1999), and Asahi Modern Craft Exhibition, Tokyo/Osaka (2000). She has been a member of the Japan Craft Design Association since 2000.

The quiet silence I and II, brooches, 1995
5.6 × 5.6 × 0.3 cm
Silver, gold leaf, lead leaf, inlaid work

Aya Nakayama was born in Tokyo in 1946. She studied industrial design at the Tokyo National University of Fine Arts and Music and graduated in 1969. In 1973 she established her own studio, specializing in jewellery design. She has been included in several international group exhibitions, including *Contemporary Japanese Crafts* in Frankfurt (1992) and *Japanese Studio Crafts* at the Victoria and Albert Museum, London (1995). She was awarded the grand prix at the International Jewellery Art Exhibition, Tokyo, in 1976 and in 1989 she received the 'Promotion Award' at the Japan Design Competition, Ishikawa Prefecture.

Aya **Nakayama**

Hug, **brooch pin 2 and 3, 2001**
11 × 7 × 5 cm
11 × 7.5 × 7 cm
Foamed plastics, linen, *urushi*

Nobuko Nishiwaki was born in Tokyo.
She studied Japanese literature at Shirayui
Women's College before pursuing a
career in jewellery design. Since 1982
she has taken part in competitions, both
in Japan and throughout Europe; she won
the 'Fine Work Award' at the International
Pearl Design Contest, Tokyo, in 1987
and again at the Japan Jewellery Art
Exhibition, Tokyo, in 1992. Her work
has been acquired for the permanent
collection of the Kestner Museum
in Hanover, Germany.

Brooch, 1998
3.8 × 8 × 9.4 cm
Natural stone, 24k gold, 18k gold brooch pin,
reinforced by sheets of fibreglass

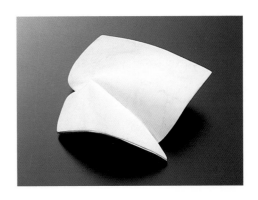

Nobuko **Nishiwaki**

Brooches, 1998
3.8 × 8 × 9.4 cm
3.8 × 9.6 × 9.5 cm
4 × 6.9 × 8.4 cm
Natural stone, 24k gold, 18k gold brooch pin,
reinforced by sheets of fibreglass

I was fortunate to come across cardboard, which I use for the following reasons.
It is cheap, non-precious, popular and nowadays of standard manufacture from factories.
There is nothing special about it. It's easy for everyone to find all over the world, and
because we use it as packaging it never attracts people's attention for itself. Its destiny
is to be thrown away after people have used it, and so it is totally different from
Japanese paper, which is very beautiful and artistic in itself.
I was fascinated and inspired by the idea of making it into jewellery and how I might give
it power, brilliance, dignity and grace. It also offers many things to discover and
possibilities to explore.
The most difficult part of the process of making cardboard jewellery is the cutting down
of the layered mass by hand. It's not easy to cut down a fine piece to my liking. I'd
already tried to use every imaginable cutting instrument, but I couldn't find one that
satisfied me in every respect. So recently I've started to use this disadvantage to create
new modes of expression.

Ritsuko Ogura

Red cardboard brooches, 1994
11.5 × 4.5 × 2.5 cm
13 × 4.5 × 3 cm
Cardboard, acrylic colour, silver

Ritsuko **Ogura**

Ritsuko Ogura was born in Osaka in 1951
and studied English and American
literature at Tezukayama Junior College,
graduating in 1972. From 1983 she has
taken part in the International Jewellery
Art Exhibition, Tokyo, and Japan Jewellery
Art Exhibition, Tokyo, eight times, and her
work has also been shown in Yugoslavia
at the International Jewellery Exhibition
(1985), at the Triennale Européene du
Bijou in Paris (1990), and at the Japanese
Contemporary Exhibition in Spello, Italy
(1996). More recently, Ogura has exhibited
at *Schmuck* 1999 and 2000 in Munich.

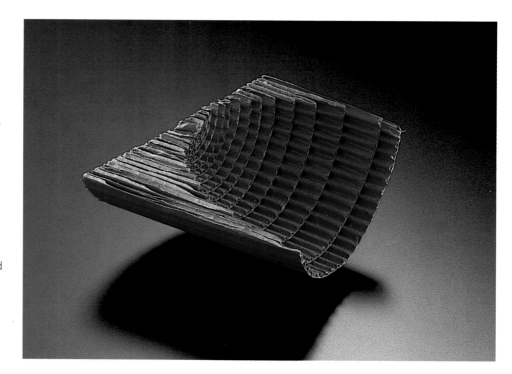

Red cardboard pin brooch, 2000
8.5 × 7.5 × 3.5 cm
Cardboard, acrylic colour, silver

Masafumi Sekine was born in Saitama Prefecture in 1949. He graduated in jewellery and metal carving from the Tokyo National University of Fine Arts and Music in 1978. In 1982, Masafumi received the Prize for Excellence at the Japanese Craft Exhibition, Tokyo, and the Tansui-oh Award for young metalwork artists at the Satoh Foundation in 1987. He has taken part in several group exhibitions, notably *Japanese Studio Crafts* at the Victoria and Albert Museum, London, in 1995, and since 1991 has held annual solo exhibitions in Nihonbashi.

Masafumi **Sekine**

Keribori Brooch I, 1996
Katakiri Brooch II, 1997
Kebori Brooch III, 1997
Marukebori Brooch IV, 1997
2.6 × 9 × 0.6 cm
Silver

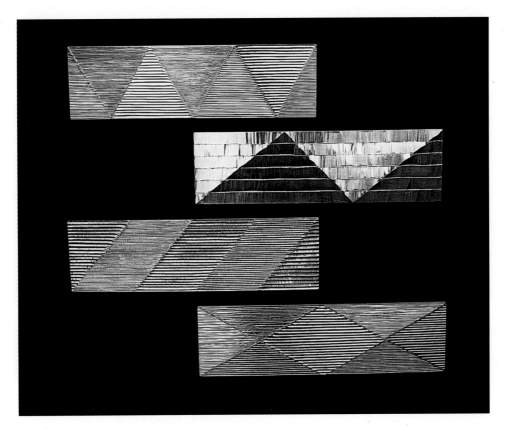

Keiko Sera was born in Hiroshima in 1955. She studied model-making at Tokyo's Women's Junior Art College, graduating in 1986. Since 1991 she has taken part in group exhibitions around the world, including *Jugendgestaltet* in Munich (1993), where she won the Fine Works Award, *Contemporary Japanese Craft and Jewelry Design* in Los Angeles (1996) and *Japanese Contemporaries* at the Lesley Craze Gallery in London (1999).

***Clouds*, brooch, 1999**
16 × 8 × 2 cm
Enamel, cloth, brass

I worked at a *cloisonné* studio (I now specialize in *yusen-shippou*), and I gradually became fascinated by the vivid colours that *shippou* can produce. In addition, I started trying to incorporate cloth, especially patches of old kimono given to me by my grandmother.
Keiko Sera

Keiko **Sera**

Clouds, necklace, 1996
45 × 21 × 4 cm
Enamel, cloth, brass

January, brooch, 1996
9 × 7 × 2 cm
Enamel, cloth

Chieko Shimizu was born in 1947 in Yamanashi Prefecture. She studied craft design at Musashino Junior College of Art and Design and graduated in 1968. First exhibiting at the International Jewellery Art Exhibition, Tokyo, in 1983, Shimizu has taken part in several group shows, including *Jewellery Today Japan* in Trondheim, Norway (1991) and *Contemporary Japanese Craft and Jewelry Design* in Los Angeles (1996). Since 1991 she has held a series of solo exhibitions in Tokyo, and her work can also be seen at the Museum of Earrings in Gunma, Japan, where it is in a permanent collection.

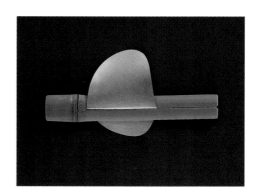

Clip brooch 1, 1995
12 × 6 × 0.5 cm
Soot-covered bamboo, 834 gold

Chieko **Shimizu**

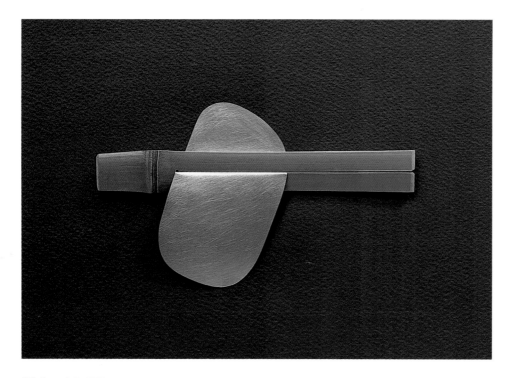

Clip brooch 2, 1995
12 × 7 x 0.5 × cm
Soot-covered bamboo

I use *susu* bamboo, whose colour has turned dark brown from being part of an inglenook fireplace for over 100 years. I can make an interesting colour contrast between this and eighteen-carat gold sheet. By utilizing the elastic qualities of bamboo I am able to create jewellery without using pins or other metal equipment for attaching the jewellery to the body/garments. I characterize my work through the act of clipping; for example, clipping jewellery on to clothes or earrings on to ears.

I aim to create simple but sophisticated works. I have been practising *sadô* (the art of tea making) since I was ten years old and I am inspired by its refined and intense air.

Chieko Shimizu

Haruko Sugawara was born in 1951 in Tokushima Prefecture. She now lives and works in Saitama Prefecture. She graduated from Musashino Art University in 1971 and has since taken part in several group exhibitions and been selected for several crafts competitions. In 1973 she won silver prize at the International Pearl Design Contest, Tokyo, and in 1996 won the grand prix at the Japanese Jewellery Arts Competition.

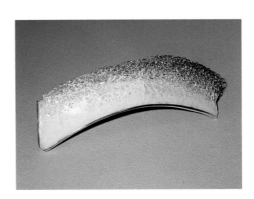

Brooch, 1995
2 × 10 × 4 cm
Gold, silver, enamel

Haruko **Sugawara**

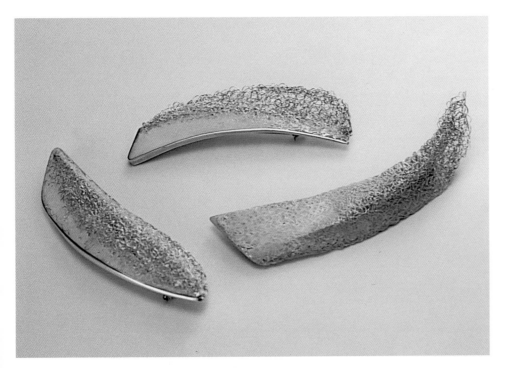

Brooches, 1995
2 × 10 × 4 cm
2 × 12 × 4 cm
Gold, silver, enamel

Rings, 2000

5 × 4.8 × 2.3 cm

Silver

Hiroko Sugiyama was born in 1955 in Tokyo. In 1975 she began to study jewellery under Minato Nakamura. Her work, which makes use exclusively of silver, has been exhibited internationally since 1984, notably in Germany (1987), Norway (1991) and Los Angeles (1996). In 1985 she was awarded a prize at the 6th International Jewellery Competition of the Schmuckmuseum Pforzheim, Germany.

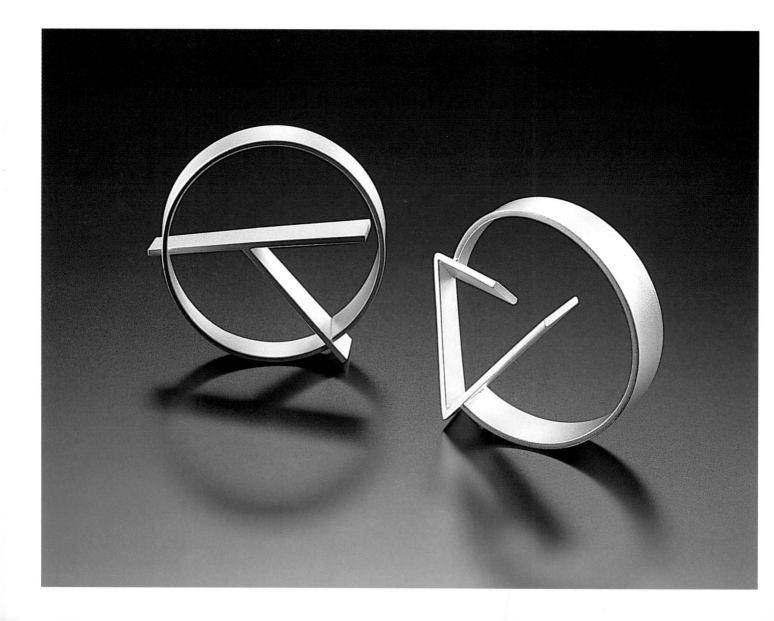

Rings, 2000
6 × 3.2 × 6 cm
Silver

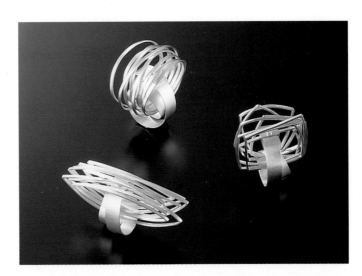

Hiroko **Sugiyama**

Rings, 1998
2.4 × 2 × 2.6 cm
Silver

I am greatly attracted to very subtle materials, such as extremely thin wires or metal sheets, metal leaf or transparent tree sap. When confronted by, for example, a thick metal sheet, I become overwhelmed by its strong physical presence and am unable to react or to make physical contact with it. On the other hand fine wires and sheets, metal leaf and sap have appeal enough despite their physical subtlety.

Although a single wire or sheet might not be strong enough for a piece of jewellery, when it is united with others, with careful inspection at each stage of the process, the material becomes strong and expressive, in a different way from a chunk of metal.

The greatest advantage is that the weight of the object does not increase substantially even when its size becomes much larger.

As my father is a craftsman–jeweller I grew up in an environment where the sound of the hammer and files was always heard. For me, being involved in the creation of jewellery is a natural consequence and part of my daily life.

Emiko Suo

Heartbeat, necklace, 2000
1.2 × 16 × 60 cm
Stainless steel, silver

Heartbeat, necklace, 2000
1.2 × 16 × 60 cm
Stainless steel, silver

Emiko Suo was born in Tokyo in 1966. She specialized in silversmithing at the Tokyo National University of Fine Arts and Music, graduating in 1992. Since then, Suo has taken part in numerous group and solo exhibitions, both in Japan and Europe, including the *Internationale Handwerksmesse* in Munich, where she has exhibited three times since 1994; *Contemporary Japanese Jewellery* in Ghent, Belgium (1995), and *Jewellery Moves* at the National Museums of Scotland, Edinburgh, in 1998. She has won several awards over the years and in 1995 her work was acquired by the Munich State Museum for Applied Arts.

Emiko **Suo**

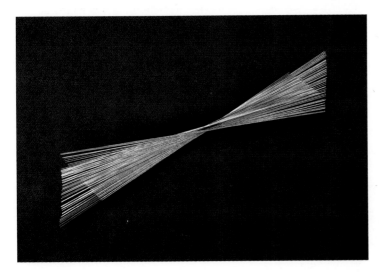

Brooch, 2000
5 × 30 × 5 cm
Stainless steel, gold leaf

Endless, bracelet, 2001
6.5 × 11 × 9.5 cm
Aluminium, gold leaf, copper

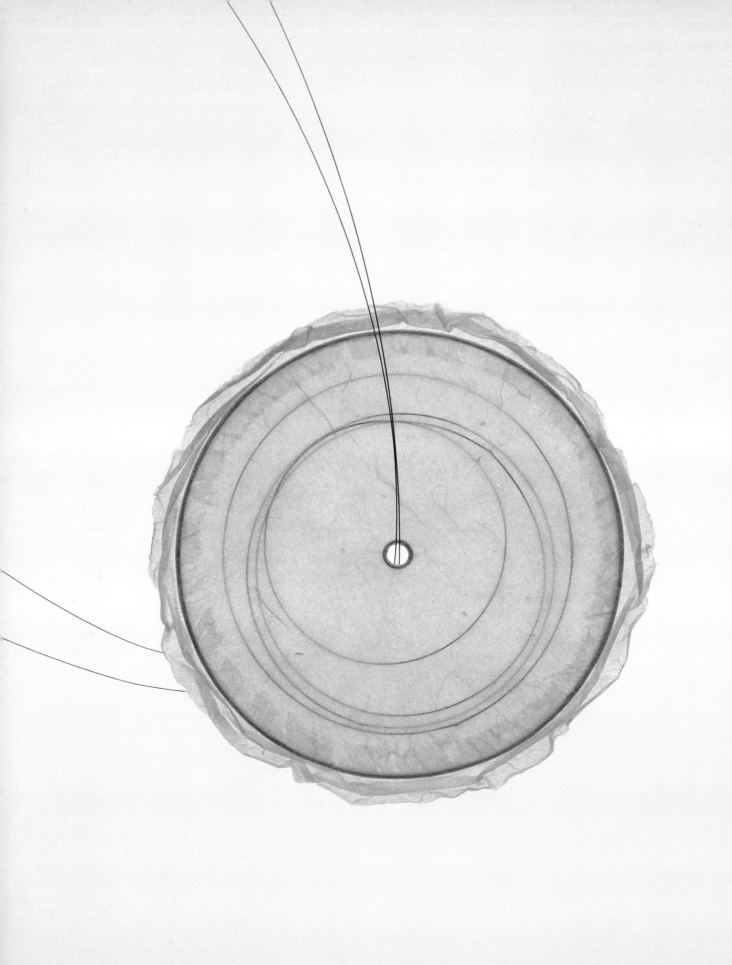

Metal and Washi, necklace, 1999

60 × 12 × 0.3 cm

Washi, silver, brass, gold

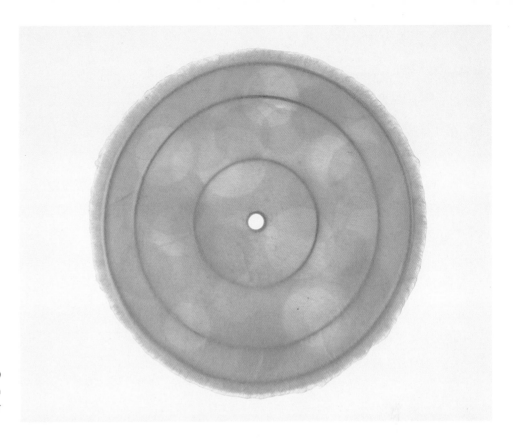

Metal and Washi, pendant head, 1999

12 × 12 × 0.3 cm

Washi, silver

Eiji **Suwa**

Metal and Washi, pendant heads, 1999

12 × 12 × 0.3 cm

Washi, silver

Eiji Suwa was born in 1978 in Gunma Prefecture. He graduated from the advanced jewellery design product course at Hiko Mizuno College of Jewellery in Tokyo in 2000, but stayed there one more year to complete a research training programme. In 1999 he was awarded a prize at the International Craft Exhibition in Itami. His work revolves around combining metal, which he calls a "cold, inorganic" material, with *washi* (Japanese paper), which is handmade and so, according to Suwa, "possesses warmth". In bringing these together, he aims to neutralize the opposites and create jewellery that provides relief.

Ear ornament, 1998
0.3 × 3 × 5 cm
18k gold, acrylic resin

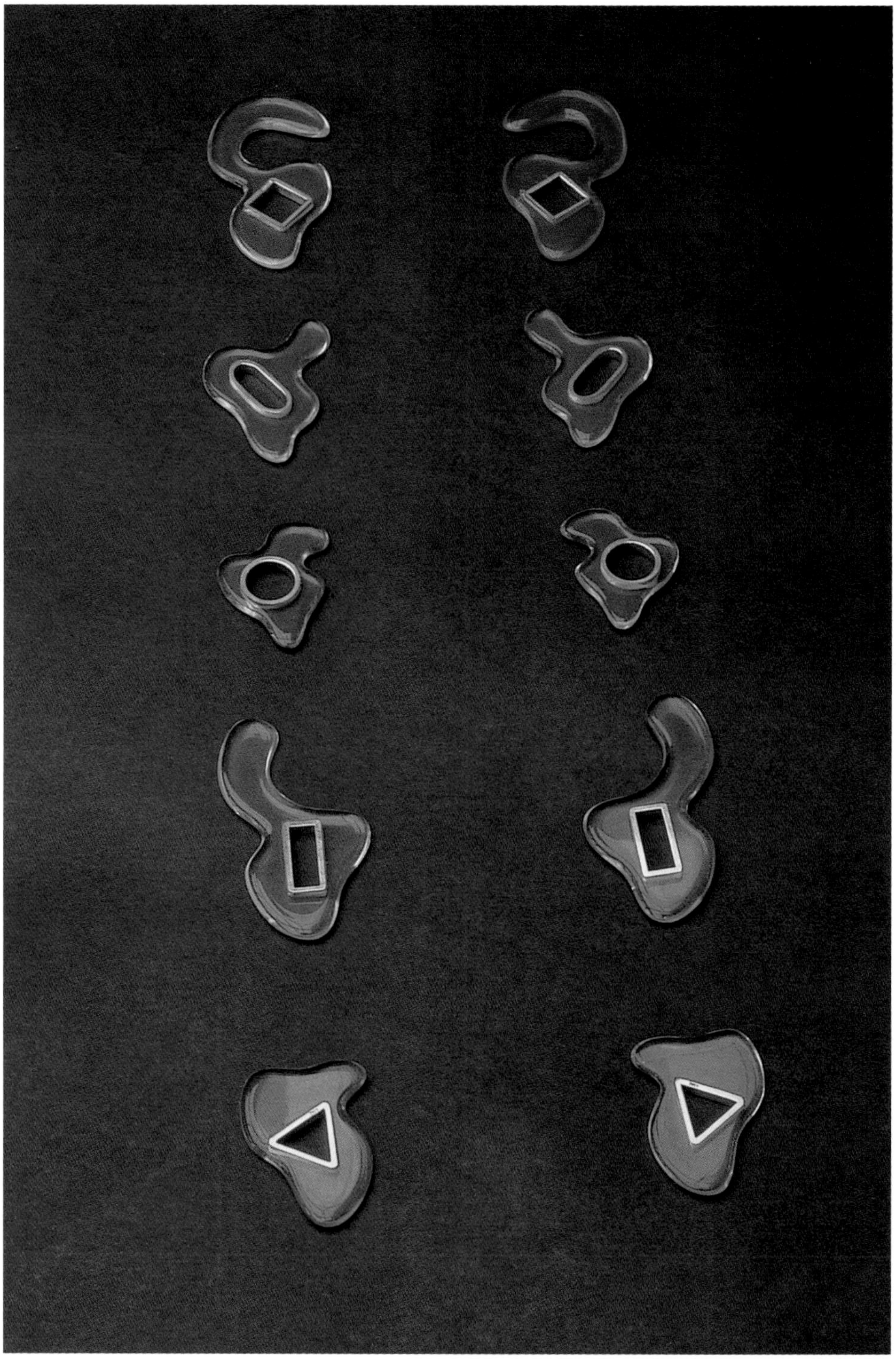

Masaki Takahashi was born in 1969.
He studied metal carving to postgraduate
level, graduating in 1997 from the Tokyo
National University of Fine Arts and Music,
but staying to become Technical Assistant
in 1999. As a student, he received several
prizes in shows including the Graduation
Exhibition in 1995, the Japanese Jewellery
Art Competition, Tokyo, in 1996, and in
1997 the Kanazawa Arts and Crafts
Competition and the Japan Gold and
Silver Works Exhibition, Tokyo. He has
taken part in several group exhibitions
travelling to Germany and Austria in 1999.

Masaki **Takahashi**

Ear ornament, 1998

0.3 × 3 × 5 cm

18k gold, silver, acrylic resin

Neckpiece, 1998
45 × 70 × 13 cm
Newspaper, adhesive, matt varnish

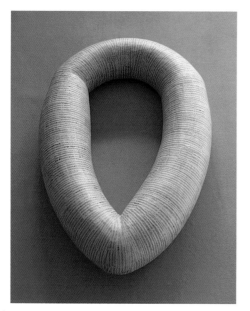

Neckpiece, 1998
45 × 70 × 13 cm
Newspaper, adhesive, matt varnish

Neckpiece (detail), 1998
45 × 70 × 13 cm
Newspaper, adhesive, matt varnish

Kana Takenaka was born in 1971. In 1992
she graduated from Saga Junior College
of Art. Her work is characterized by the
use of newspaper, adhesive and varnish
in a traditional Japanese paper technique,
hariko.

Kana **Takenaka**

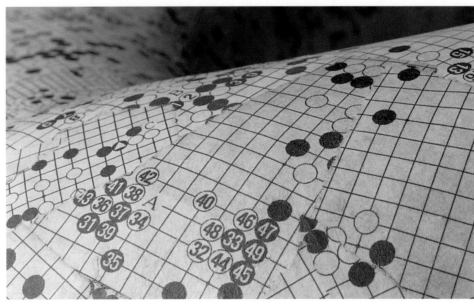

Neckpiece, 1998
55 × 45 × 14 cm
Newspaper, adhesive, matt varnish

Neckpiece (detail), 1998
55 × 45 × 14 cm
Newspaper, adhesive, matt varnish

Showzi Tsukamoto was born in Saitama Prefecture in 1946. He specialized in metal craft and in 1968 graduated from the Tokyo National University of Fine Arts and Music, winning the Salon de Printemps Award for best graduate work. Since 1972 he has been president of design company Zivaco Inc., specializing in interior, exterior and jewellery design. His work is characterized by the use of the traditional craft technique *urushi* (Japanese lacquer work) alongside contemporary materials, such as aluminium and titanium. In 1989 he was awarded the Louis Vuitton Moët Hennessey Science pour L'Art award for exceptional artwork.

(Enrin) The Connecting Cycles: Vermilion,
necklace, 2000
18 × 18 × 2 cm
Iron, 24k gold foil, *urushi* coating on a metal substrate

I have always been fascinated by traditional Japanese crafts, especially arms and armour from the fourteenth to eighteenth centuries. *The Aesthetics of the Tea Ceremony* by Kobori Enshu (1579–1647) inspired me as well. When I was a student the concepts and design techniques of William Morris (1834–1896) were important to me.
Showzi Tsukamoto

Showzi **Tsukamoto**

***(Enrin) The Connecting Cycles: Gold*, necklace, 2000**
18 × 18 × 2 cm
Iron, 24k gold foil, *urushi* coating on a metal substrate

Kyoko Urino was born in Ashikaga, Tochigi Prefecture, and studied three-dimensional design at Central St Martins College of Art and Design in London, graduating in 1992, followed by a master's degree in metalwork at the State University of New York, graduating in 1993. Urino has held solo exhibitions in Japan since 1995, when she showed at the Inui Gallery in Ashikaga and the Gallery IF in Tokyo. She was presented with the Design for Gold Award at Goldsmiths' Hall in London in 1992, and a merit award at the Associated Artists Gallery in Illinois in 1994.

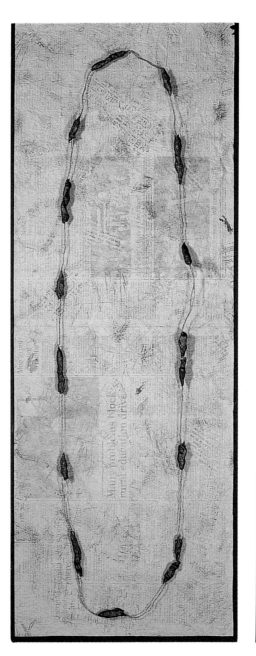

Eternal Life # 1203, necklace, 1999
Length 150 cm
Frame 78 × 30 × 0.5 cm
Japanese paper, low (untreated silk), *kakishibu* (persimmon) stain

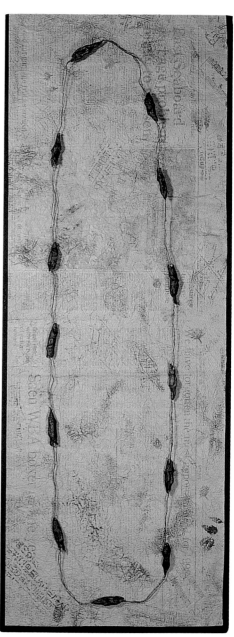

Eternal Life # 427, necklace, 1999
Length 150 cm
Frame 78 × 30 × 0.5 cm
Japanese paper, low (untreated silk), *kakishibu* (persimmon) stain

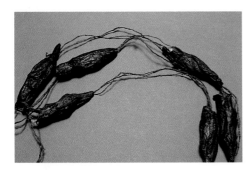

Eternal life #1203, **necklace (detail), 1999**

Length 150 cm

Frame 78 × 30 × 0.5 cm

Japanese paper, low (untreated) silk, *kakishibu*

(persimmon) stain

Kyoko **Urino**

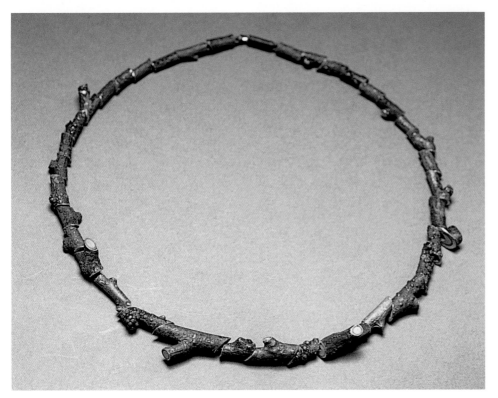

Nature study series, **necklace #1, 1999**

Length 43 cm

Frame 25 × 25 × 4 cm

Twigs, electroforming, patination

***Breast Ornament*, 1994**
7.5 × 43 × 35 cm
Copper, silver plate

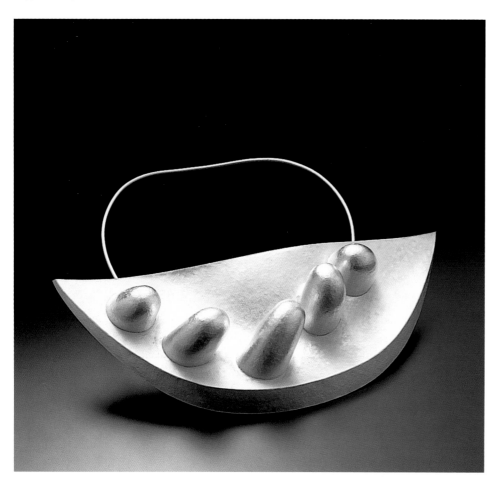

Mizuko Yamada was born in Tokyo in 1964 and studied extensively at the Tokyo National University of Fine Arts and Music, first taking a BA, then an MA, and finally graduating as a research student in 1992. That year she held a solo show at Gallery f-air Ginza in Tokyo and participated in the group exhibition *Jewellery Art* at the Japan Jewellery Designers Association, Tokyo, going on to appear in a string of shows, mainly around Tokyo. In 1995 she visited the UK to take up a residency at the Royal College of Art, London, and again in 1997 as an artist-in-residence at Edinburgh College of Art.

I started making my bigger jewellery pieces using copper for economic reasons. I have worked with copper for a long time during my studies so it is easy for me. I originally started silver plating my copper pieces to get a general idea of what they'd look like in silver. But I began to realize that the colour of silver-plated copper with a matt finish achieved by hammering is different from the colour of silver itself. It is whiter, lighter, cleaner and has a warmer tone. I am very satisfied with this colour range so I have made many pieces this way.

My inspiration for making jewellery is working with the metal itself. I have been studying metal as a material for a long time now. It is my basic inspiration, along with my great interest in the organic forms of humans, animals and plants. The five senses are also a very important part of my work: they are my main inspiration, and I am interested in making jewellery that stimulates them.

Mizuko Yamada

Tactile, bracelet, 1998
11 × 8.5 × 8.5 cm
Copper, silver, raising, soldering, silver plate

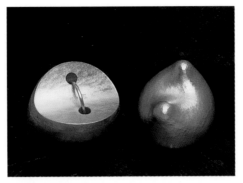

Tactile, ring, 1999
4.5 × 4.5 × 3.7 cm
Silver, raising, soldering

Bracelet (with sake cup form), 1992
8.5 × 15 × 15 cm
Copper, burnt Japanese lacquer, gold leaf,
raising, welding

Mizuko **Yamada**

Bracelet, 1992
11 × 17 × 18 cm
Copper, silver plate

Bracelet, 1992
12.5 × 6 × 13.5 cm
Copper, silver plate

Tactile, bracelet, 2000
8.2 × 11.5 × 11.5 cm
Copper, silver, raising, welding, silver plate

***Kojiki (Mythology of Nation)*, brooch, 1994**
5.3 × 4.6 × 0.8 cm
18k gold, jade, chasing, soldering

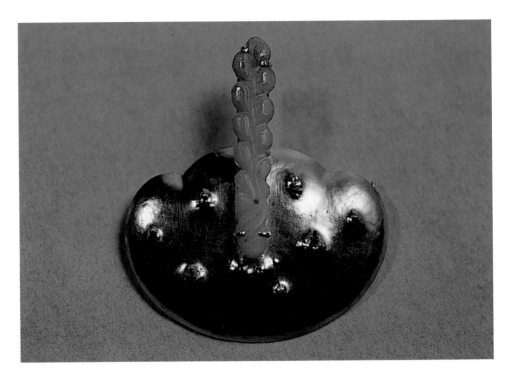

Reiko Yamada was born in Tokyo in 1933.
In 1958, she graduated from the Tokyo
National University of Fine Arts and Music,
when she was awarded the Salon de
Printemps Prize by the Japanese Ministry
of Education. From 1988 to 1995 she was
President of the Japan Jewellery
Designers Association and since 1958 has
taken part in several group shows in
Tokyo. To date she has held two solo
exhibitions: in 1991 at the Gallery IF, and
in 1998 at the AC Gallery, both in Tokyo.

Reiko **Yamada**

Kojiki (Mythology of Nation), brooch, 1994
7 × 4.6 × 1.5 cm
18k gold, blue topaz

IC Pin Brooches, 1999
1.6 × 2.1 × 1.75 cm
Silver, IC computer part

Esmé Turid Yamaguchi was born in New York in 1962. She graduated from the State Academy of Music in Munich in 1984 and gained basic jewellery-making skills while studying flute repair and flute making at Japanese flute manufacturer Sankyo. In 1995 she went on to study jewellery design with Minato Nakamura in Tokyo. Since 1996 she has exhibited in a series of group shows in Japan, including the International Craft Exhibition in Itami (1999) and the travelling exhibition *Men's Elegance*, which visited Tokyo, Okayama, Nagoya and Sapporo in 2000.

Esmé Turid **Yamaguchi**

Genki Brooches, 1995–96
2.5 × 14 × 13.3 cm
Silver, plastic reflector

I am influenced by various trends in contemporary society, such as the inundation of computer-related technology into seemingly every facet of existence. Although I have been fascinated by the resultant multitude of new materials, I've also felt a deepening anxiety at this onslaught and the increasing distancing of nature and spirit from thought. The latter phenomenon has been a particularly strong influence in my most recent work, in which one of my main aims has been to try and express a sense of radiating positive cosmic energy and motion.
Esmé Turid Yamaguchi

Most importantly, I have always been surrounded by textiles since the very beginning of my life. Cloth is the closest and most familiar material in people's lives; however, because of that, it is likely to be overlooked. Cloth as a material can offer friendly and somewhat commonplace feelings.

There are always possibilities to be found by using new materials or processes. However, this is not the priority of my work. For me, concentrating on the pursuit of new elements can be dangerous.

I never practised or studied the production of jewellery. I understand that my involvement in *Contemporary Japanese Jewellery* is due to the fact that people have perceived and appreciated jewellery-like qualities in my works. I learned the skills of *edo-yuzen* (one of Japan's oldest dyeing techniques) at university. I am due to start working in the field of jewellery this year and I am currently undertaking preparatory study.

It is difficult to point to exactly where my inspiration comes from; however, I tend to create works that reflect on the act of capturing moments and elements from daily life to extract the essence of the whole. I find myself intrigued by the fact that people lead lives.

Masaki Yamamoto

Untitled 2, 1994
12 × 18 × 1.4 cm
Cotton, dye, pigment, fake leather

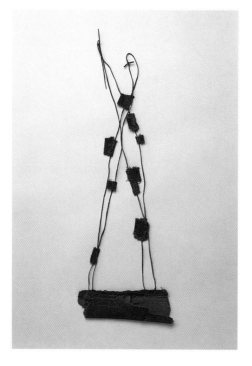

Untitled 3, 1993
4.5 × 8.2 × 1 cm
Cotton, dye, pigment, fake leather

Masaki Yamamoto was born in Hiroshima in 1959. He graduated from the department of craft at the Tokyo National University of Fine Arts and Music in 1985, and stayed to complete a postgraduate course in fine-art studies in 1987. Since 1993 he has held solo shows in galleries in Tokyo and Kyoto, and taken part in several group exhibitions around the world, including *Contemporary Textiles: Miniature Work from Japan*, which toured Belgium and Australia in 1998. Yamamoto has also exhibited twice at *Façon Japon* in Lyons, in 2000 and 2001.

Masaki **Yamamoto**

Untitled 1, 1993
30 × 4.7 × 0.5 cm
Cotton, dye, pigment, fake leather

Untitled 5, 1996
11 × 5.2 × 3 cm
Cotton, dye, pigment, fake leather

Untitled 4, 1996
24 × 5 × 1.5 cm
Cotton, dye, pigment, fake leather

Urushi, which is produced only in Asian countries, is an earth-friendly, natural material, and its techniques have been developed greatly in Japan.
Shinya Yamamura

Brooch '98-12, 1998
7 × 6 × 2 cm
Urushi, deer hair, *tamenuri*

Shinya Yamamura was born in Tokyo in 1960. He studied extensively at Kanazawa College of Art, finally graduating in 1986, but returning in 1992 to work there as Assistant Professor. His work, which is characterized by the use of *urushi*, a traditional Japanese lacquer-work technique, has been widely exhibited in both solo and group shows around the world. Yamamura's jewellery can also been seen in the permanent collections of the Victoria and Albert Museum, London, and the National Museums of Scotland, Edinburgh.

Shinya **Yamamura**

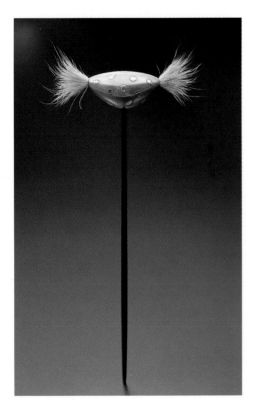

Kanzashi 1–6, 2000
20 × 5.5 × 4.5 cm
Urushi, gold, silver, eggshell, brass, deer hair

Brooch '96-03, 1996
9 × 5.5 × 3 cm
Urushi, gold, *hyomon*

I develop work inspired by words and sentences. I search for ways of representing incorporeal entities and give them shape in my work. I used photographs for one of my recent works, which originated from a personal desire. I do not generally like photography, because my first impressions or feelings evoked by the actual scenery, for example, are often spoilt in photographic images. Nevertheless, I once wished to capture those feelings as much as possible; I felt like grasping a piece of sky or clouds and keeping it in my own pocket in order to feel satisfied. I made a piece of jewellery using an image of the sky for myself to wear in order to feel at one with the scenery.

Various people and things have always influenced me to a certain extent, but not particular figures or works. I mentally accumulate casual conversations and interactions and develop them in my works. For me, inspiration always lies in ordinary spaces, within myself and my everyday life.

Sae Yoshizawa

Rings, 2000
11 × 6 × 6 cm
Photograph, silver, gum, glass beads, thread

Sae Yoshizawa was born in 1977 in Kanagawa Prefecture, and now lives and works in Kamakura. She studied at Hiko Mizuno College of Jewellery in Tokyo, graduating in 1998. The following year, she was invited to show at the International Craft Exhibition in Itami. Her work since she left college has focused on the repeated use of several elements: photographs, rubber, silicone cord, glass, wood, stone and hemp.

Sae **Yoshizawa**

Bracelets, 2000
8 × 11 × 11 cm
Photograph, gum

List of Works

The following is a list of works included in the exhibition. Most of these are illustrated in the preceding pages.

NOBUKO ABE

Irogane, brooch, 1998
6 x 6 x 1.5 cm
Silver 950, *shakudo*, *shibuichi*, *hagiawase zougan*

Irogane, brooch, 1998
11 x 3.5 x 3 cm
Silver 950, *shakudo*, copper, *hagiawase zougan*

Check on the Brooch, brooches, 1999
5.3 x 4.8 x 1.5 cm
5.8 x 4.3 x 1.5 cm
6 x 4.3 x 1.5 cm
Silver 950, *shakudo*, gold foil 999.9, *nunome zougan*

TERUO AKATSU

Catch Illusion, ring, 1993
1 x 2.9 cm
Dust, gold plate, silver

Illusion dust, brooch, 1993
Length 30 cm
Dust, stainless-steel wire, nickel silver

Illusion dust, necklace, 1993
35 x 35 cm
Dust, stainless-steel wire

Necklace, 1994
24 x 24 x 1 cm
Roof tile

MIKIKO AOKI

Bracelet, 1993
13 x 18 x 18 cm
Felted wool

YASUKO ARAI

A Moment, brooches, 1996
0.5 x 7 x 7 cm
0.5 x 7.5 x 7.5 cm
18k gold, 950 silver, *shakudo kiribame zougan*

A Moment, rings, 1998
4.5 x 2.8 x 4 cm
5 x 2.8 x 4 cm
Silver, *niello*

A Moment, rings, 1998
5.3 x 3 x 1.5 cm
24k gold, 950 silver, *niello*

TOMOMI ARATA

Treasures from Under the Sea, ring 1, 1997
2.5 x 2 x 1 cm
Hand-cast silver, enamel, glass, sand, clear stone

Treasures from Under the Sea, ring 2, 1997
3.8 x 2 x 1.5 cm
Hand-cast silver, enamel, glass, sand, purple stone

KYOKO FUKUCHI

Echo of Time of Past, brooches, 2000
4.8 x 5 x 3 cm
5 x 5 x 3.4 cm
7.3 x 7.3 x 0.7 cm
Hemp paper

HIROMASA HASHIMOTO

Ruten, necklaces, 1999
24 x 24 x 4 cm
Silver, silicone cord

YUTA HATAYA

Metal Cell, ring, 1998
2.4 x 2.4 x 0.83 cm
Silver, copper

Metal Fibre, ring, 1999
2.7 x 2.3 x 0.4 cm
Silver, *kuromido*

Metal Fibre, ring, 1999
2.8 x 2.3 x 0.4 cm
Silver, copper

Wa, ring, 2000
3.75 x 3.75 x 0.4 cm
Silver, copper

MASAKO HAYASHIBE

A River Flows, necklace, 1994
72 cm
Silk, pearls, platinum

Rhizome (neckwear I and II), 1998
4 x 14 x 2 cm
Diameter 13 cm
Glass beads, fishing thread

Rhizome (bracelet III), 1998
Diameter 7.5 cm
Glass beads, fishing thread

KOZO HIRAMATSU

Expansion, brooches, 2000
13 x 13 x 5 cm
13.5 x 13 x 3.5 cm
Copper, gold leaf

YASUKI HIRAMATSU

Brooch K20, 1998
5.6 x 5.4 x 2.5 cm
Gilding

Necklace, 1998
19 x 20 x 7 cm
Aluminium, gold leaf

Brooch, 1999
14.9 x 2.5 x 1.6 cm
950 silver and gold plate, gold leaf

Necklace, 1999
27 x 27 x 10 cm
950 silver and gold plate

Brooch K24, 2000
4.6 x 4.2 x 1.6 cm
Silver, gilding

ICHIRO IINO

Ring, 1992
9 x 9 x 4 cm
18k gold, Japanese paper, gold leaf

Brooches, 1997
7.2 x 2.6 x 1.5 cm
8.3 x 2.5 x 1 cm
8.5 x 2.6 x 1.7 cm
Silver, amalgam, gilding, marble

Ring, 1997
4.5 x 2.7 x 4 cm
Silver, amalgam, gilding, marble

Brooches, 1999
7.6 x 2.3 x 0.85 cm
Silver, Pt 900, amalgam, gilding

HIROKI IWATA

Antiquity, brooch, 1999
4.5 x 6.5 x 0.8 cm
Silver, enamel, 18k gold, gold foil, silver leaf

Black, brooch, 1999
6 x 4.5 x 0.8 cm
Silver, enamel, gold foil, gold leaf

Green, brooch, 1999
2 x 12 x 0.9 cm
Silver, enamel, silver foil, silver leaf

White, necklace, 1999
9.5 x 3.5 x 1 cm
Silver, enamel, 18k gold, silver foil

Necklace, 2001
Diameter 23 cm
Silver, enamel

KIMIAKI KAGEYAMA

Suzushita, brooch, 2001
2 x 4 x 9 cm
Urushi, hemp, resin, mineral pigments (black), gold paint

The Heart, brooch, 2001
1.5 x 6.8 x 9.3 cm
Urushi, hemp, resin, mineral pigments (black), gold paint

TORU KANEKO

Shoulder brooches 1–9, 1994
5 x 4.5 x 4.5 cm
Silver

YOSHIE KOBA

Time fading away, necklace, 1993
110 x 40 x 10 cm
Traditional Japanese paper, bisque fired

Time fading away, brooch, 1994
22 x 17 x 8 cm
Traditional Japanese paper, bisque fired

Time fading away, necklace, 1994
130 x 20 x 5 cm
Traditional Japanese paper, bisque fired

Necklace, 1998
25 x 20 x 5 cm
Traditional Japanese paper, bisque fired

SHINICHIRO KOBAYASHI

Point of Contact, 1993
3 x 2 x 2 cm
5 x 4 x 1 cm
5 x 4 x 1 cm
Pure, cast gold

White Dew, necklace, 1994
32 x 15 x 2 cm
Camphor, stainless-steel wire

TAKASHI KOYAMA

Brooches, 1995
2 x 9 x 1.3 cm
2 x 9.5 x 1.2 cm
2 x 9.6 x 1.2 cm
2.4 x 9.5 x 1 cm
2.4 x 9.9 x 1.2 cm
Silver, gold

Necklace, 1998
3.5 x 23 cm diameter
Silver, gold

Necklace, 1998
3.5 x 23 cm diameter
Silver, platinum

An Apartment, brooches, 1999
3 x 12.6 x 1.1 cm
4.9 x 6.6 x 1.1 cm
5.1 x 3.3 x 1.1 cm
6.5 x 4.7 x 1.1 cm
8.8 x 5.5 x 1.1 cm
9.1 x 5.6 x 1.1 cm
9.5 x 7.4 x 1.1 cm
Silver, gold

HIROYUKI MASHIKO

Rouge, necklace, 1994
1.2 x 36 x 36 cm
Carmine, 950 silver, chromium plate

MITSUO MASUDA

Brooch
7.3 x 4.5 x 1 cm
Silver, gold, ruby, chasing, *katakiri* carving, mercury gilding

Ring
2 x 1.5 x 2.4 cm
Silver, chasing, soldering

Ring
2.4 x 1.5 x 3 cm
Silver, garnet, filing, soldering

TOMOMI MATSUNAGA

Beni (carmine), bracelet, 2001
7 x 9 x 7 cm
Linen, metal-leaf paint

Natural bamboo bracelet, 2001
7.5 x 8 cm
Bamboo

Natural bamboo necklace, 2001
8 x 15 x 24 cm
Bamboo

Silver Coil, bracelet, 2001
6.5 x 6 x 4.5 cm
Linen, metal-leaf paint

SAKURAKO MATSUSHIMA

Breast ornament, 2000
44 x 24 x 5.5 cm
Urushi, hemp cloth, Mexican abalone, gold powder, tin powder

Necklace, 2000
26 x 24 x 1.5 cm
Urushi, eucalyptus leaves, hemp cloth, Mexican abalone, gold powder, tin powder

Upper-body ornament, 2000
64 x 53 x 10 cm
Urushi, hemp cloth, Mexican abalone, mother-of-pearl, gold powder, leather

MAYUMI MATSUYAMA

Bracelets, 1996
7 x 22 x 22 cm
Leather

Caterpillar, necklaces, 1999
4.5 x 32 x 32 cm
Leather

MIKIKO MINEWAKI

One de wan, bracelet, 1999
2 x 7 x 6 cm
Miso soup bowl

One de wan, ring, 1999
1 x 2.8 x 3 cm
Miso soup bowl

Pla-ring, rings, 2000
3 x 2.5 x 1 cm
Disposable lighter

KAZUKO MITSUSHIMA

Ring, 1988
3 x 5 x 1 cm
Blown glass, 22k gold

Ring, 1990
5.5 x 3 x 2.5 cm
Glass, 24k gold

Ring, 1998
3 x 3 x 1.8 cm
Glass, silver

Ring, 1998
4.5 x 3.5 x 2 cm
Glass, platinum

Ring, 1998
5 x 3 x 2.8 cm
Glass, 18k gold

Necklace, 2000
20 x 14 x 1 cm
Blown glass, silver, nylon

Ring, 2000
5 x 4 x 1 cm
Glass

Brooch, 2001
6 x 6 x 1 cm
Blown glass

Necklace, 2001
16 x 14 x 2.5 cm
Blown glass, 18k gold

Necklace, 2001
16 x 14 x 3 cm
Blown glass, silver

BENIKO MOTONAGA

Colours, 1999
57 x 99 cm
Resin

NORIKO NAGANO

Neckpiece I, 1994
110 x 10 x 3 cm
Urethane rubber

Neckpiece II, 1996
60 x 60 x 0.5 cm
Urethane rubber

NAGI NAKAJIMA

Ori-Kite, brooch, 1998
3 x 9 x 8.5 cm
Silver

Ori-Spiral, bangle, 1999
3.5 x 7 x 6.5 cm
Gold

Ori-Spiral, bangle, 1999
3.5 x 7 x 6.5 cm
Silver

Ori-Spiral, rings, 2000
2.5 x 2 cm diameter
2 x 2 cm diameter
1.7 x 2 cm diameter
Gold

MINATO NAKAMURA

Out of Joint, rings, 1994
4.9 x 2 x 3.3 cm
5 x 3 x 3.2 cm
5.2 x 1.4 x 3.3 cm
5.5 x 2.1 x 2.1 cm
5.5 x 3.2 x 2 cm
(Above pieces loaned by the National Museum of Modern Art, Tokyo)
4.9 x 3.2 x 2 cm
5 x 3.2 x 3 cm
5 x 3.5 x 2.2 cm
5.5 x 2.1 x 2.1 cm
3.5 x 3.2 x 1.6 cm
Silver

Bracelet, 1999
5 x 6 x 5.5 cm
Silver

Brooch, 1999
4 x 8.4 x 6 cm
Silver

RYUICHIRO NAKAMURA

Unforgettable Shine, necklace, 2001
42 x 52 x 7 cm boxed
Saw blade, pins, specimen box

KAORU NAKANO

The quiet silence I and II, brooches, 1995
5.6 x 5.6 x 0.3 cm
Silver, gold leaf, lead leaf, inlaid work

The quiet silence III and IV, 1997
6 x 6 x 0.1 cm
3.5 x 7 x 0.1 cm
Silver, gold leaf, lead leaf, inlaid work

AYA NAKAYAMA

Hug, brooch pins 1, 2, 3 and 4, 2001
11.5 x 7 x 5.5 cm
11 x 7 x 5 cm
11 x 7.5 x 7 cm
10 x 8.5 x 4 cm
Foamed plastics, linen, *urushi*

NOBUKO NISHIWAKI

Brooches, 1998
3.8 x 8 x 9.4 cm
3.8 x 9.6 x 9.5 cm
4 x 6.9 x 8.4 cm
Natural stone, 24k gold, 18k gold brooch pin, reinforced by sheets of fibreglass

RITSUKO OGURA

Red cardboard brooches, 1994
13 x 4.5 x 3 cm
Cardboard, acrylic colour, silver

Burnt cardboard brooch, 1999
13 x 13 x 3 cm
Cardboard (burnt), silver

Burnt cardboard brooch, 1999
14 x 5.5 x 2.5 cm
Cardboard (burnt), acrylic colour, silver

Thin cardboard brooches, 2000
12 x 10 x 3.5 cm
21 x 8.5 x 3.7 cm
Cardboard, silver

Red cardboard brooch, 2001
5.8 x 5.6 x 5.7 cm
Cardboard, acrylic colour, silver
(Private Collection)

MASAFUMI SEKINE

Keribori Brooch I, 1996
2.6 x 9 x 0.6 cm
Silver

Katakiri Brooch II, 1997
2.6 x 9 x 0.6 cm
Silver

Kebori Brooch III, 1997
2.6 x 9 x 0.6 cm
Silver

Marukebori Brooch IV, 1997
2.6 x 9 x 0.6 cm
Silver

KEIKO SERA

Clouds, necklace, 1996
45 x 21 x 4 cm
Enamel, cloth, brass

January, brooch, 1996
9 x 7 x 2 cm
Enamel, cloth

Red snapper, brooch, 1997
10 x 6.5 x 2 cm
Enamel, cloth, glass

Clouds, brooch, 1999
16 x 8 x 2 cm
Enamel, cloth, brass

CHIEKO SHIMIZU

Clip brooch 1, 1995
12 x 6 x 0.5 cm
Soot-covered bamboo, 834 gold

Clip brooch 2, 1995
12 x 7 x 0.5 cm
Soot-covered bamboo

HARUKO SUGAWARA

Brooches, 1995
2 x 10 x 4 cm
2 x 12 x 4 cm
Gold, silver, enamel

HIROKO SUGIYAMA

Rings, 1998
2.2 x 3.5 x 2.5 cm
2.4 x 2 x 2.6 cm
4 x 2.5 x 2.5 cm
Silver

Rings, 2000
4 x 3.2 x 8 cm
5 x 4.8 x 2.3 cm
5 x 5 x 2.2 cm
6 x 3.2 x 6 cm
6 x 3.5 x 5.2 cm
Silver

EMIKO SUO

Brooch, 2000
5 x 30 x 5 cm
Stainless steel, gold leaf

Heartbeat, necklace, 2000
1.2 x 16 x 60 cm
Stainless steel, silver

Brooch, 2001
11 x 2.4 x 2 cm
Aluminium, gold leaf, copper

Endless, bracelet, 2001
6.5 x 11 x 9.5 cm
Aluminium, gold leaf, copper

EIJI SUWA

Metal and Washi, necklace,
1999
60 x 12 x 0.3 cm
Washi, silver

Metal and Washi, necklace,
1999
60 x 12 x 0.3 cm
Washi, silver, brass, gold

Metal and Washi, pendant
head, 1999
12 x 12 x 0.3 cm
Washi, silver

Metal and Washi, pendant
head, 1999
12 x 12 x 0.3 cm
Washi, silver, brass

Metal and Washi, pendant
heads, 1999
12 x 12 x 0.3 cm
Washi, silver, gold

MASAKI TAKAHASHI

Ear ornaments, 1998
0.3 x 3 x 5 cm
18k gold, acrylic resin

Ear ornaments, 1998
0.3 x 3 x 5 cm
18k gold, silver, acrylic resin

KANA TAKENAKA

Neckpiece, 1998
45 x 70 x 13 cm
Newspaper, adhesive, matt
varnish

Neckpiece, 1998
55 x 45 x 14 cm
Newspaper, adhesive, matt
varnish

SHOWZI TSUKAMOTO

*(Enrin) The Connecting Cycles:
Gold*, necklace, 2000
18 x 18 x 2 cm
Iron, 24k gold foil, *urushi*
coating on a metal substrate

*(Enrin) The Connecting Cycles:
Vermilion*, necklace, 2000
18 x 18 x 2 cm
Iron, 24k gold foil, *urushi*
coating on a metal substrate

KYOKO URINO

Eternal life #427, necklace,
1999
Length 150 cm
Frame 78 x 30 x 0.5 cm
Japanese paper, low (untreated
silk), *kakishibu* (persimmon)
stain

Eternal life #1203, necklace,
1999
Length 150 cm
Frame 78 x 30 x 0.5 cm
Japanese paper, low (untreated
silk), *kakishibu* (persimmon)
stain

Nature study series, necklace
#1, 1999
Length 43 cm
Frame 25 x 25 x 4 cm
Twigs, electroforming,
patination

MIZUKO YAMADA

Bracelet (with sake cup form),
1992
8.5 x 15 x 15 cm
Copper, burnt Japanese lacquer,
gold leaf, raising, welding

Tactile, bracelet, 1998
11 x 8.5 x 8.5 cm
Copper, silver, raising,
soldering, silver plate

Tactile, ring, 1999
4.5 x 4.5 x 3.7 cm
Silver, raising, soldering

Tactile, bracelet, 2000
8.2 x 11.5 x 11.5 cm
Copper, silver, raising, welding,
silver plate

REIKO YAMADA

Sighing of Trees, brooch, 1991
9.1 x 8.6 x 2.1 cm
Silver, chasing, soldering

Kojiki (Mythology of Nation),
brooch, 1994
7 x 4.6 x 1.5 cm
18k gold, blue topaz

Kojiki (Mythology of Nation),
brooch, 1994
5.3 x 4.6 x 0.8 cm
18k gold, jade, chasing,
soldering

ESMÉ TURID YAMAGUCHI

Genki Brooch, 1995
2.5 x 14 x 13.3 cm
Silver, plastic reflector

Genki Brooch, 1996
2.5 x 13.5 x 12.7 cm
Silver, plastic IC sheet

Genki Brooch, 1996
2.5 x 14 x 13 cm
Silver, plastic tubing, metallic
sheet

IC Pin Brooches, 1999
1.2 x 1.2 x 2.2 cm
1.3 x 1.8 x 1.9 cm
1.35 x 1.9 x 2.4 cm
1.4 x 1.6 x 2.1 cm
1.4 x 1.8 x 1.7 cm
1.4 x 1.8 x 2.5 cm
1.4 x 1.95 x 1.6 cm
1.4 x 1.95 x 2.4 cm
1.4 x 2.1 x 1.9 cm
1.45 x 1.9 x 2.05 cm
1.5 x 1.85 x 2.5 cm
1.5 x 2.2 x 2.1 cm
1.5 x 2.25 x 1.8 cm
1.6 x 2.1 x 1.75 cm
1.8 x 2.8 x 2 cm
Silver, IC computer part

MASAKI YAMAMOTO

Untitled 1, 1993
30 x 4.7 x 0.5 cm
Cotton, dye, pigment, fake
leather

Untitled 3, 1993
4.5 x 8.2 x 1 cm
Cotton, dye, pigment, fake
leather

Untitled 2, 1994
12 x 18 x 1.4 cm
Cotton, dye, pigment, fake
leather

Untitled 4, 1996
24 x 5 x 1.5 cm
Cotton, dye, pigment, fake
leather

Untitled 5, 1996
11 x 5.2 x 3 cm
Cotton, dye, pigment, fake
leather

SHINYA YAMAMURA

Brooch '96-03, 1996
9 x 5.5 x 3 cm
Urushi, gold, *hyomon*

Brooch '97-08, 1997
7 x 7 x 3.2 cm
Urushi, red lacquer

Brooch '98-12, 1998
7 x 6 x 2 cm
Urushi, deer hair, *tamenuri*

Kanzashi 1–6, 2000
20 x 5.5 x 4.5 cm
Urushi, gold, silver, eggshell,
brass, deer hair

SAE YOSHIZAWA

Bracelets, 2000
8 x 11 x 11 cm
Photograph, gum

Rings, 2000
11 x 6 x 6 cm
Photograph, silver, gum, glass
beads, thread

Glossary

atelier
Small design and workshop space, normally associated with one particular artist or group of artists.

black *shibuichi*
Copper alloy: more than 75% copper (see *shibuichi*).

bonsai
Trees dwarfed by pruning and displayed in small containers. Bonsai has the status of an art form, with some of the trees outlasting several generations of artists.

British Craft Centre
An organization founded to promote modern crafts in Britain and abroad. The forerunner of the Crafts Council.

camphor
A white crystalline resin from Asian and Australian laurels, often used to repel moths.

chokin
Literally 'metal hammering'. Covers the techniques called 'raising', 'forming', 'chasing' and 'repoussé' in the West. Still practised to a very high standard in Japan.

cloisonné
An enamelling technique whereby small, metal-walled cells are filled with enamel and then filed back after firing to give a characteristically smooth surface.

Cordoba leather
High-quality, Spanish, decorated leather and leather goods.

Gerda Flockinger
A post-war jeweller and influential teacher working in Britain with a distinctive style based on surface treatment of gold set with precious and semi-precious stones.

Goldsmiths' Hall
A historical building housing the headquarters of the London City Livery Company, founded in the twelfth century and associated with the gold, silversmithing and jewellery industries in Britain. Responsible for 'assaying', the testing and hallmarking of precious-metal items.

gold leaf
Very thin, fine sheets of beaten gold used for gilding or embedding.

hemp cloth
A coarse cloth woven from hemp (*Cannabis salvatica*). Light and durable, it was the base for some traditional lacquer vessels and armour.

hyomon
A lacquer-work technique in which thin, shaped and cut silver or gold is placed between layers of lacquer. The lacquer is then shaped to the pattern of the metal.

inlay
A technique involving cutting a groove or space into a metal surface and hammering in another metal or material to create a level surface.

irogane
Copper alloyed with a variety of metals to achieve different effects.

kanji
Chinese character used in Japanese writing.

Kanji Hashimoto collection
An important recent collection of historical jewellery, largely from Europe with some pieces from Japan and other cultures. Mainly assembled through auction-house purchases, it includes some distinguished early English jewellery.

kimono
A garment constructed from a number of different elements, essentially ankle-length with a sash and wide sleeves. A kimono is symbolic of traditional Japan.

kiribame zougan
A technique of cutting and inlaying that uses a solder-type inlay.

kurimodo
A traditional Japanese alloy-based copper with some impurities of metal which give a brown-black colouring like that of *shakudo*.

Kyoto
An ancient city, once the royal capital of Japan until the court moved to Tokyo. It is associated with important religious shrines and temples, and a certain refined, reserved and understated style, born chiefly of aristocratic impoverishment.

Meiji
The name given to the era in the nineteenth century when modernization occurred, or Meiji restoration. The name is lent to culture and artefacts fashionable during this period.

mercury gilding
One of the most ancient ways of gilding metal, not much practised in the West, partly as a result of plating but also because its practice can be highly dangerous to the artist. Gold is dissolved in mercury to form a paste that coats the metal object. The mercury is boiled away, leaving a particularly fine and durable surface. Commonly practised in Asia on religious objects.

Mingei
A cultural movement committed to the collection and preservation of traditional folk arts.

niello
Alloy of gold, silver, lead and sulphur.

Onchi Zuroku
Pattern books illustrating designs or decorative schemes considered suitable by the government for development by craftsmen for international export.

origami
The art of folding paper to create forms both practical and decorative.

persimmon
Several different tropical hardwood trees with large edible orange fruits.

raku
A ceramic object fired using a reductive process that gives a distinctive texture to the surface of the glaze.

roof tile
Traditional Japanese roof tiles, often made of a grey-coloured clay, have a characteristic wave shape, with the tiles used for edging the roof ornamented by a circular, detailed boss. Used mainly now for temples and royal premises.

shakudo
Copper alloy: 95% copper, 5% gold.

shibuichi
Copper alloy: 75%, 25% silver.

Shinto
Japan's official religion, involving the worship of a number of ethnic divinities associated with gods of the earth and nature.

tamenuri
A lacquer-work technique in which a coloured lacquer base is covered with a layer of clear or matt lacquer.

Ukiyo-e
Woodblock prints created by the artist chiselling into wood to create a negative image. Often featuring important or fashionable views, or portraits of well-known figures.

urushi
The traditional Japanese lacquer-work technique, employing sap from the sumac tree, used all over Asia as a varnish to provide a smooth surface with a deep shine. Lacquer was imported to Japan and has enjoyed several centuries of development to become an art particularly associated with Japanese culture. It is a highly poisonous material, and lacquering has to take place in a very humid environment to enable drying.

washi
Handmade paper using cloth fibres or plant material, and offering different qualities of translucency or texture.

water and willow worlds
Colloquial names for geisha and hostess communities and businesses.

white *shibuichi*
Copper alloy: more than 25% silver (see *shibuichi*).

yusen-shippou
A type of enamelling in which thin silver plate is used to divide the colours.

Bibliography

Amsterdam–München–Amsterdam–Tokyo–Amsterdam–Tokyo–München–München, exhib. cat., ed. Otto Kunzli, Amsterdam, Munich and Tokyo, 1987

Takahiko Mizuno, Kimiaki Kageyama and Fumio Ishizaki, *Jewellery Bible*, Tokyo, 1996

Jewellery 99: International Craft Exhibition, exhib. cat., Itami, Museum of Crafts, 1999

Jewelleryquake, exhib. cat., Tokyo, Hiko Mizuno College of Jewellery, 1994

8th Biennial Japan Jewellery Designers Exhibition, exhib. cat., Tokyo, 1999

Jewellery Art, exhib. cat., Sapporo, Sapporo Art Park, 1998

UR Jewellery Association 35th Anniversary Exhibition, exhib. cat., Tokyo, 1994

'96 Jewellery Art Competition, exhib. cat., Itami and Tokyo, 1996

Japanese Crafts 2000, exhib. cat., Tokyo, Osaka and Fukuoka, 2000

The Art of Rings: From Ancient Egypt to the 20th Century, exhib. cat., by Diana Scarisbrick, Tankosha Publishing, 2000

Harada Katzutoshi, Director of the Metal Department, 'From Metal Fittings for Swords to Jewellery Making: The Achievements of Matsumura Manzaburo', *Jewellery Design Guide*, Tokyo, 2000

Contemporary Jewellery: Exploration by Thirty Japanese Artists, exhib. cat., ed. Masami Shiraishi and Toyojiro Hida, Tokyo, National Museum of Modern Art, 1995

Jewellery Today Japan: Japan Today in Scandinavia, exhib. cat., Tokyo, Trondheim and Bergen, 1991

Four Seasons of Jewellery, bi-monthly magazine, ed. Noriko Takagi, Tokyo

Index

Author Acknowledgements and Picture Credits

Organizing an international, transcultural exhibition creates many demands, and numerous people in both Japan and Europe have given freely of their time and information to help me curate this exhibition.

I must express my debt to Reiko and Mizuko Yamada, whose kindness, enthusiasm, energy and knowledge enabled the exhibition to grow as it has. From the Crafts Council, Louise Taylor gave me the chance to realize my idea, while the exhibitions team have all been fantastically supportive of it.

I am grateful to Dr Senju Satoh, President of the Satoh Foundation, who enabled artists' pieces to journey across the globe, and to Toyojiro Hida, of the National Museum of Modern Art, for his fascinating essay.

Central St Martins College of Art and Design funded my original research trip to Japan and colleagues there and at the Buckinghamshire Chilterns University College have been gracious in the face of the disruption that organizing an exhibition entails.

Jenny and Michio Harada have kindly put up with my endless phone calls for advice.

Also in Tokyo, I was greatly helped by Takeshi Sakurai from the British Council, Emeritus Professor Yasuki Hiramatsu and Professor Ichiro Iino from the Tokyo National University of Fine Arts and Music, President Takahiko Mizuno, Professor Kimiko Kageyama and all my friends at the Hiko Mizuno College of Jewellery, and Noriko Tagaki, editor of the *Four Seasons of Jewellery* magazine.

Finally I would like to thank the artists who have given their precious time to answer my many requests and enquiries and allowed us to use their work and voices.

This project would not have been possible without the support of Geoff Palmer.

The illustrations in this book have been reproduced by kind permission of the following:

Key top: t; bottom: b; left: l; right: r; centre: c.

Mikiko Aoki p. 31 bl, p. 40; Yasuko Arai p. 32 tr, p. 36 br, p. 41; Tomomi Arata p. 31 bcl, p. 42, p. 43; Kyoko Fukuchi p. 30 tl, p. 44, p. 45; Hiromasa Hashimoto p. 34 tc, p. 46, p. 47; T. Hatakeyama p. 28 br, p. 37 bl, p. 71; Yuta Hataya p. 33 bl, p. 48, p. 49; Masako Hayashibe p. 34 bcr, p. 50, p. 51; Kozo Hiramatsu p. 32 bl, p. 52, p. 53; Yasuki Hiramatsu p. 13 t, p. 18 bl, p. 32 tl, p. 54, p. 55; Ichiro Iino p. 32 br, p. 56; Hiroki Iwata p. 31 br, p. 57; Kimiaki Kageyama p. 28 bc, p. 37 t, p. 58, p. 59, back cover (left); Toru Kaneko p. 34 tl, p. 37 bc, p. 60, p. 61; Yoshie Koba p. 29 br, p. 62, p. 63; Shinichiro Kobayashi p. 19 bc, p. 35 tc, p. 64, p. 65; Takashi Koyama p. 17 b, p. 33 tl, p. 66; Sara Morris p. 12 b; Hiroyuki Mashiko p. 1, p. 14 t, p. 35 bl, p. 36 t, p. 67; Sakurako Matsushima p. 28 tr, p. 72, p. 73; Mayumi Matsuyama p. 31 tc, p. 74, p. 75; Mikiko Minewaki p. 19 t, p. 21, p. 29 bc, p. 76, p. 77; Kazuko Mitsushima p. 78; Beniko Motonaga p. 29 bl, p. 79; Nagi Nakajima p. 18 br, p. 33 bc, p. 82, p. 83; Minato Nakamura p. 17 t, p. 33 tr, p. 84, p. 85; Ryuichiro Nakamura p. 35 r, p. 86; Kaoru Nakano p. 32 tc, p. 87; Aya Nakayama p. 28 tl, p. 88; Nobuko Nishiwaki p. 34 br, p. 89; Hitoshi Nishiyama p. 16, p. 30 br, p. 33 br, p. 37 br, p. 90, p. 110, p. 111 bl, bc, back cover (right); Katsunori Otsuka p. 32 bc, p. 36 bl, p. 38; Masafumi Sekine p. 8 c, p. 15, p. 33 tc, p. 91; Keiko Sera p. 31 bcr, p. 92, p. 93; Chieko Shimizu p. 29 tl, p. 94; Toshio Sugano p. 12 t; Haruko Sugawara p. 31 tr, p. 95; Hiroko Sugiyama p. 34 bl, p. 96, p. 97; Emiko Suo p. 34 blc, p. 98, p. 99; Eiji Suwa p. 30 bl, p. 100, p. 101; Swarovski p. 23; Masaki Takahashi p. 19 br, p. 35 bc, p. 102, p. 103; Fumio Takashima p. 8 r, p. 29 tc, p. 80, p. 81, front cover; Kana Takenaka p. 19 bl, p. 30 bc, p. 104, p. 105; Tokyo National University of Fine Arts and Music Collection p. 11 t; Showzi Tsukamoto p. 28 bl, p. 106, p. 107; Kyoko Urino p. 30 tr, p. 36 bc, p. 108, p. 109; Mizuko Yamada p. 8 l, p. 11 b, p. 68, p. 69, p. 111; Reiko Yamada p. 13 b, p. 34 tr, p. 112, p. 113; Esmé Turid Yamaguchi p. 29 tr, p. 114, p. 115; Masaki Yamamoto p. 31 tl, p. 116, p. 117; Shinya Yamamura p. 2, p. 28 tc, p. 118, p. 119; Sae Yoshizawa p. 30 tc, p. 120, p. 121.